Games of Ancient Rome

Titles in The Way People Live series include:

Cowboys in the Old West
Games of Ancient Rome
Life Among the Great Plains Indians
Life Among the Ibo Women of Nigeria
Life Among the Indian Fighters
Life Among the Pirates
Life Among the Samurai
Life Among the Vikings
Life During the Black Death
Life During the Crusades
Life During the French Revolution
Life During the Gold Rush
Life During the Great Depression
Life During the Middle Ages
Life During the Renaissance
Life During the Russian Revolution
Life During the Spanish Inquisition
Life in a Japanese American Internment Camp
Life in a Medieval Castle
Life in Ancient Athens
Life in Ancient Greece
Life in Ancient Rome
Life in an Eskimo Village
Life in a Wild West Show
Life in Charles Dickens's England
Life in the Amazon Rain Forest
Life in the American Colonies
Life in the Elizabethan Theater
Life in the Hitler Youth
Life in the North During the Civil War
Life in the South During the Civil War
Life in the Warsaw Ghetto
Life in Victorian England
Life in War-Torn Bosnia
Life of a Roman Slave
Life of a Slave on a Southern Plantation
Life on a Medieval Pilgrimage
Life on an Israeli Kibbutz
Life on Ellis Island
Life on the American Frontier
Life on the Oregon Trail
Life on the Underground Railroad
Life Under the Jim Crow Laws

Games of Ancient Rome

by Don Nardo

Lucent Books, P.O. Box 289011, San Diego, CA 92198-9011

Library of Congress Cataloging-in-Publication Data

Nardo, Don, 1947–
Games of ancient Rome / by Don Nardo.
p. cm. — (the way people live series)
Includes bibliographical references (p.) and index.
Summary: Discusses life in ancient Rome, focusing on the origin and popularity of public games, Rome's monumental game facilities, gladiators, wild animal shows, and other spectacles.
ISBN 1-56006-655-5 (lib. bdg. : alk. paper)
1. Games—Rome—Juvenile literature. 2. Games—History—Juvenile literature. [1. Games—Rome. 2. Rome—History.] I. Title. II. Series: Way People Live.
GV31.N37 2000
790'.0937—dc21 99-33783
CIP

Printed in the U.S.A.

Contents

Foreword

Discovering the Humanity in Us All

Books in The Way People Live series focus on groups of people in a wide variety of circumstances, settings, and time periods. Some books focus on different cultural groups, others, on people in a particular historical time period, while others cover people involved in a specific event. Each book emphasizes the daily routines, personal and historical struggles, and achievements of people from all walks of life.

To really understand any culture, it is necessary to strip the mind of the common notions we hold about groups of people. These stereotypes are the archenemies of learning. It does not even matter whether the stereotypes are positive or negative; they are confining and tight. Removing them is a challenge that's not easily met, as anyone who has ever tried it will admit. Ideas that do not fit into the templates we create are unwelcome visitors—ones we would prefer remain quietly in a corner or forgotten room.

The cowboy of the Old West is a good example of such confining roles. The cowboy was courageous, yet soft-spoken. His time (it is always a he, in our template) was spent alternatively saving a rancher's daughter from certain death on a runaway stagecoach, or shooting it out with rustlers. At times, of course, he was likely to get a little crazy in town after a trail drive, but for the most part, he was the epitome of inner strength. It is disconcerting to find out that the cowboy is human, even a bit childish. Can it really be true that cowboys would line up to help the cook on the trail drive grind coffee, just hoping he would give them a little stick of peppermint candy that came with the coffee shipment? The idea of tough cowboys vying with one another to help "Coosie" (as they called their cooks) for a bit of candy seems silly and out of place.

So is the vision of Eskimos playing video games and watching MTV, living in prefab housing in the Arctic. It just does not fit with what "Eskimo" means. We are far more comfortable with snow igloos and whale blubber, harpoons and kayaks.

Although the cultures dealt with in Lucent's The Way People Live series are often historically and socially well known, the emphasis is on the personal aspects of life. Groups of people, while unquestionably affected by their politics and their governmental structures, are more than those institutions. How do people in a particular time and place educate their children? What do they eat? And how do they build their houses? What kinds of work do they do? What kinds of games do they enjoy? The answers to these questions bring these cultures to life. People's lives are revealed in the particulars and only by knowing the particulars can we understand these cultures' will to survive and their moments of weakness and greatness.

This is not to say that understanding politics does not help to understand a culture. There is no question that the Warsaw ghetto, for example, was a culture that was brought about by the politics and social ideas of Adolf

Hitler and the Third Reich. But the Jews who were crowded together in the ghetto cannot be understood by the Reich's politics. Their life was a day-to-day battle for existence, and the creativity and methods they used to prolong their lives is a vital story of human perseverance that would be denied by focusing only on the institutions of Hitler's Germany. Knowing that children as young as five or six outwitted Nazi guards on a daily basis, that Jewish policemen helped the Germans control the ghetto, that children attended secret schools in the ghetto and even earned diplomas—these are the things that reveal the fabric of life, that can inspire, intrigue, and amaze.

Books in The Way People Live series allow both the casual reader and the student to see humans as victims, heroes, and onlookers. And although humans act in ways that can fill us with feelings of sorrow and revulsion, it is important to remember that "hero," "predator," and "victim" are dangerous terms. Heaping undue pity or praise on people reduces them to objects, and strips them of their humanity.

Seeing the Jews of Warsaw only as victims is to deny their humanity. Seeing them only as they appear in surviving photos, staring at the camera with infinite sadness, is limiting, both to them and to those who want to understand them. To an object of pity, the only appropriate response becomes "Those poor creatures!" and that reduces both the quality of their struggle and the depth of their despair. No one is served by such two-dimensional views of people and their cultures.

With this in mind, The Way People Live series strives to flesh out the traditional, two-dimensional views of people in various cultures and historical circumstances. Using a wide variety of primary quotations—the words not only of the politicians and government leaders, but of the real people whose lives are being examined—each book in the series attempts to show an honest and complete picture of a culture removed from our own by time or space.

By examining cultures in this way, the reader will notice not only the glaring differences from his or her own culture, but also will be struck by the similarities. For indeed, people share common needs—warmth, good company, stability, and affirmation from others. Ultimately, seeing how people really live, or have lived, can only enrich our understanding of ourselves.

Introduction

Rome's Favorite Form of Entertainment

The Roman games, particularly the large-scale, violent spectacles such as chariot races, gladiatorial combats, and the slaughter of wild animals, constitute one of the most famous aspects of ancient Roman culture. Indeed, later ages came to view these games as uniquely Roman, a sort of trademark of Roman civilization. The violent nature of these spectacles has contributed to some modern perceptions of the Romans as a violent, callous, even a cruel people. Modern novels and movies about ancient Rome, for example, have frequently portrayed the Roman masses frenzied with blood lust as they watch humans and animals die in the arena.

Yet all of these views are either false or significantly exaggerated or oversimplified. To begin with, the often violent public games in question were not "uniquely" Roman, for the Romans did not invent these pastimes. In fact, the Romans were not an especially inventive people and more often than not tended to borrow cultural ideas and customs from other peoples. Describing this tendency of his countrymen, the Roman politician and historian Sallust (Gaius Sallustius Crispus, 86–34 B.C.) remarked:

> Our ancestors . . . were never too proud to take over a sound institution from an-

A drawing depicts the excitement felt by Roman spectators as they watched chariot races, gladiator fights, and the other events that comprised their famous games.

Pilgrims from all over Greece approach Olympia, site of the famous Olympic Games. Many Romans felt that the Greek games were too tame.

> other country. . . . In short, if they thought anything that an ally or an enemy had was likely to suit them, they enthusiastically adopted it to Rome; for they would rather copy a good thing than be consumed with envy because they had not got it.[1]

The two peoples the Romans borrowed from most often were the Etruscans, who in early Roman times lived in the Italian region north of Rome (then called Etruria, today Tuscany), and the Greeks. It was the Etruscans who originated the institution of fights to the death among gladiators. Rome likely picked up the custom of chariot racing from both the Etruscans and the Greeks.

Yet as history has shown, the Romans were not merely uninspired copiers. Indeed, they possessed an amazing talent for combining foreign ideas with their own native concepts and considerable practical skills to produce new versions suited to their own needs. And the Roman versions usually tended to be far larger in scope than the originals. Etruscan gladiators fought in small private settings before a handful of spectators, for instance, while their Roman counterparts eventually performed in huge public facilities before tens of thousands of people.

There is no doubt that most Romans also came to prefer games of a more physically dangerous and violent nature than did the Greeks. The Romans absorbed many Greek social and cultural ideas, especially after Rome's conquest of the Greek lands of the eastern Mediterranean in the second and first centuries B.C. However, except for boxing and chariot racing, most Romans had little interest in Greek athletics, in which serious injuries and death were rare. The average Roman found the running, jumping, and throwing events of the Olympics and other Greek games too tame. And even Greek boxing was too subdued for Roman tastes; Greek boxers covered their knuckles with leather thongs, while Roman boxers wore gloves studded with metal spikes.

But does this necessarily mean that the Romans were violent by nature? Some scholars suggest instead that over time they grew used to and became more accepting of, and even fascinated by, some aspects of the violence and death that were commonplace in most ancient societies. "Many factors inured [accustomed] the Roman to bloodshed," writes University of Massachusetts scholar Carlin A. Barton, including

> the practice [during wars] of decimation, in which the brave and guiltless were executed . . . along with the cowardly and guilty; mass executions of prisoners of war, deserters, and rebels; public and private executions . . . of all sorts (especially of slaves); torture of witnesses [in trials;] . . . [and] the pitiless vendetta [revenge feud between families].[2]

Two Greek wrestlers grapple naked, as was customary in Greece. By contrast, the Romans preferred to watch armed confrontations, particularly those featuring gladiators.

That many Romans were fascinated by violence, rather than themselves inherently violent, is demonstrated in part by the fact that as a rule they liked to watch, but not participate in, their public games. For a Roman citizen to actually take part in such public spectacles was viewed as improper, undignified, and socially unacceptable. This view was completely contrary to that of Greek society, which encouraged and glorified athletic participation by citizens. One reason that Romans (at least socially respectable ones) tended not to perform and compete in public is that they were, for much of their history, a conservative, austere people who placed much store in their dignity *(dignitas)* and public image. And actors, gladiators, charioteers, and other public performers were almost always considered social outcasts.[3]

For Roman men in particular, pride was an important reason not to compete in public, for they took special pride in their military prowess and considered losing in battle the ultimate disgrace. Simply put, for most Roman men, defeat in a public competition or display was too much like defeat in war. As noted scholar David Young remarks, "No Roman could stand the risk of losing such an individual test, of looking inferior in public. To do it naked in full view of one's enemies [as the Greeks did] would have made Roman blood run cold."[4] Thus, status-conscious Romans, especially members of the upper classes, who presented themselves as models of public behavior, preferred to confine their competitive spirit to the battlefield, the political sphere, and the law courts.

Nevertheless, eventually many of these men, along with Romans of all other walks of life, eagerly attended the public games, which were likely always crowded. By the first century A.D., the spectacles were far and away Rome's favorite form of entertainment. Attempting to explain their phenomenal popularity, a character in a dialogue by the great Roman historian Cornelius Tacitus (ca. A.D. 55–ca. 120) remarks, "The peculiar vices of the Romans seem to me almost to be conceived in the womb—interest in the stage and enthusiasm for gladiators and [race] horses."[5]

CHAPTER 1

How the Public Games Originated and Became Popular

The Romans did not always have their games. And once the games had been instituted, their nature and scope changed over the course of time, a commodity that Rome possessed in abundance. Indeed, ancient Roman civilization existed for perhaps fifteen centuries or more. Archaeologists believe that the first villages appeared on one or more of Rome's famed seven hills as early as 1000 B.C. (The city's traditional founding date of 753 B.C. may represent a dim recollection of the unification of these villages into one central town.) And the inhabitants of Italy still thought of themselves as Romans for almost a century after the last emperor was forced to vacate the throne in A.D. 476.

Modern historians divide this long timespan into three general eras (or kinds of government)—the Kingship, the Republic, and the Empire. The Kingship, in which kings ruled

A modern artist's reconstruction of the temple-studded Capitoline Hill in the "eternal" city of Rome in the second century A.D.

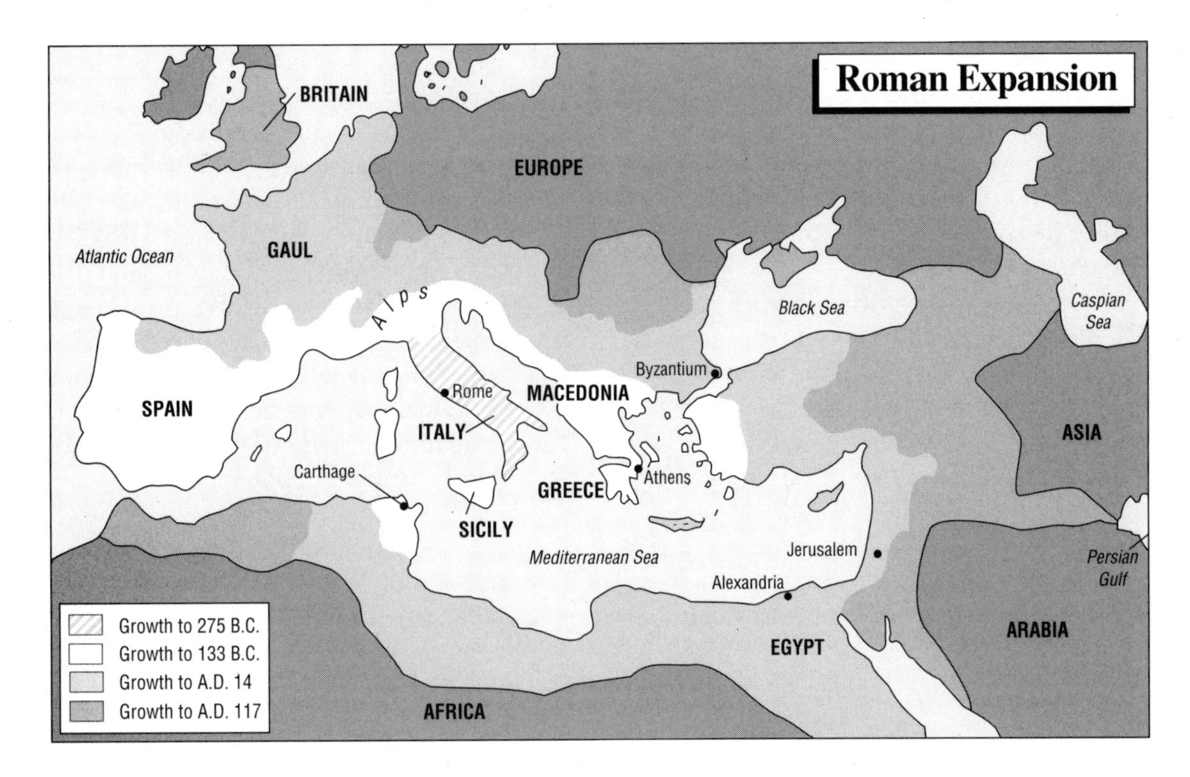

Rome, lasted until about 509 B.C., at which time the richest and most powerful landowners threw out their king and established the Republic, which had a legislature known as the Senate and elected administrator-generals called consuls. Rome then expanded outward from central Italy and by the beginning of the first century B.C. had carved out a huge realm consisting of nearly all the lands bordering the Mediterranean Sea. During that fateful century, rocked by several devastating civil wars, the Republic fell and gave way to the Empire. In 27 B.C., Octavian, undisputed victor of the final civil war, took the name of Augustus, the "exalted one," and ruled as an absolute dictator (although a highly benevolent, fair, and constructive one). It was during the late Republic and early Empire that chariot races, gladiatorial combats, and other spectacles, which had existed on a small scale in Rome for some time, became large-scale institutions sponsored almost solely by the government.

A Dislike for Athletic Games

The transition to this form of state-supported mass entertainment was not an easy one. Roman leaders were mainly aristocrats. They believed they knew what was best for the "common" people and consistently attempted to shape Roman attitudes toward watching, as well as participating in, athletic and other public competitions and performances. And at first these leaders resisted the idea of large-scale public games, fearing they would have a corruptive influence on Roman society.

This conservative, restrictive attitude was shaped to a certain degree by a general disdain for Greek games. Beginning in the 190s B.C., as Rome steadily gained control of the Greek lands, the Romans had their first major exposure to Greek athletics. The Greek games were held at the local level throughout the Greek world, and at a number of large international festivals, the most famous held every four years at Olympia, in southern Greece. These consisted of footraces, broadjumping, javelin and discus throwing, wrestling, horse and chariot races, and other events. Greeks of all social classes took part, and they customarily trained and competed in the nude.

Upper-class Romans consistently rejected Greek-style games as effeminate (unmanly) and morally decadent. The prominent first-century B.C. orator and senator Marcus Tullius Cicero expressed this typical Roman view when he quoted with approval the words of an earlier Roman writer: "To strip in public is the beginning of evil-doing."[6] Attempting to explain such apparent prudishness, the first-century A.D. Greek biographer and moralist Plutarch wrote:

> The Romans considered nothing to be the cause of the Greeks' enslavement and degeneracy as much as the gymnasia and palaestras [wrestling facilities], which gave rise to much time-wasting and laziness in the cities . . . pederasty [sex between adult men and boys], and the ruination of the youths' bodies through sleep, strolls, exercises, and precise diets, because of which they stopped practicing with weaponry and were happy to be called nimble and wrestlers and handsome instead of hoplites [warriors] and good horsemen.[7]

Roman dislike of Greek games softened somewhat in the early Empire (ca. 30 B.C.–A.D. 180) as a few of the emperors instituted their own

Greek athletes engage in various kinds of exercises and leisure games in the athletic field of a local gymnasium. Many Romans viewed Greek athletics as unmanly.

Augustus Caesar (pictured with his wife Livia), who staged the Actian Games to celebrate a military victory.

versions of Olympic competitions. The first emperor, Augustus, for example, founded the Actian games to celebrate his victory over Antony and Cleopatra in the Battle of Actium in 31 B.C.; Nero, the egotistical fifth emperor, established the "Neronian" games in Rome in the 60s A.D.; and circa A.D. 132, the emperor Hadrian, an avid admirer of Greek culture, attempted to replace the games held at Olympia with a new festival in Athens (a move that failed when most Greek athletes, out of reverence for tradition, refused to attend).

During these years, some Roman citizens began attending such athletic games along with the Greeks. Yet most leading Romans continued to promote the puritanical idea that such attendance was a symptom of society's moral decay. Tacitus summarized this view in his commentary on Nero's games:

> Traditional morals, already gradually deteriorating, have been utterly ruined by this imported laxity! . . . Foreign influences demoralize our young men into shirkers, gymnasts, and perverts. Responsibility rests with emperor and Senate. They have given immorality a free hand [by approving and staging such games]. . . . It only remains to strip and fight in boxing-gloves instead of joining the army. . . . This vileness continues even at night! Good behavior has no time left for it. In these promiscuous crowds [of spectators], debauchees [sex maniacs and perverts] are emboldened to practice by night the lusts they have imagined by day.[8]

"Bread and Circuses"

At first, many Romans, especially those in the upper classes, harbored a similar contempt for Roman games. As late as the early first century B.C., most leading Romans argued that all such public displays promoted public laziness. Moreover, they argued, holding large-scale games in the capital city might pose a threat to public order. The Romans observed many public holidays (at least fifty-seven by the early first century B.C.). Much work was suspended on some (although not all) of these holidays, so large numbers of poor urban Romans were idle during these times. Many senators and other leaders harbored the paranoid fear that if the so-called mob had too little to occupy its time it might protest, riot, or even rebel. Especially dangerous, in this view, was allowing large numbers of commoners to congregate in one place, since it might lead to civil disturbances and the erosion of state authority; consequently, the Senate long refused to approve the construction of large, permanent theaters and amphitheaters.

Nero's Games

This colorful description of the various games presented by the infamous emperor Nero (reigned A.D. 51–68), including several Greek-style athletic events, is from the first/second–century B.C. historian Suetonius's *Lives of the Twelve Caesars.*

"He gave an immense variety of entertainments—coming-of-age parties, chariot races in the Circus, stage plays, a gladiatorial show—persuading even old men of consular rank, and old ladies, too, to attend the coming-of-age parties. He . . . actually raced four-camel chariots! At the Great Festival, as he called the series of plays devoted to the eternity of the Empire, parts were taken by men and women of both Orders [i.e., the two most prestigious social classes, the patricians and knights; most members of these classes viewed this as undignified]; and one well-known knight rode an elephant down a sloping tight-rope. . . . Throughout the Festival, all kinds of gifts were scattered to the people—1,000 assorted birds daily, and quantities of food parcels; besides vouchers [coupons] for grain, clothes, gold, silver, precious stones, pearls, paintings, slaves . . . ships, blocks of city apartments, and farms. The gladiatorial show took place in a wooden theater, near the Campus Martius ["Field of Mars," a large open area near the Tiber River] . . . but no one was allowed to be killed during these combats, not even criminals. He did, however, make 400 senators and 600 knights, some of them rich and respectable, do battle in the arena. . . . He staged Pyrrhic performances [Greek precision dances] by certain young Greeks, to whom he presented certificates of Roman citizenship when their shows ended. . . . He inaugurated the Neronia, a festival of competitions in music, gymnastics, and horsemanship, modeled on the Greek ones and held every five years. . . . Nero descended to the orchestra, where the senators sat, to accept the wreath [prize] for Latin oratory and verse, which had been reserved for him by the unanimous vote of all the distinguished competitors. The judges also awarded him the wreath for a lyre solo, but he bowed reverently to them, and said: 'Pray lay it on the ground before Augustus's statue!'"

The arrogant and self-centered emperor Nero frequently sponsored public games, including athletic competitions and gladiator fights.

Citizens mill about the Roman Forum while acrobats (foreground) entertain.

As public games became increasingly popular, however, these fears proved groundless. Roman leaders found, in fact, that public spectacles, controlled by aristocrats and/or the state, could actually be potent tools for maintaining public order, and for gaining public support as well. In the Republic's waning years, upper-class Romans learned that putting on lavish spectacles was an effective way to win votes, and in the early imperial years, when elections no longer determined leadership, the emperors used the shows to bolster their personal popularity.

Therefore, the public games became part of a deliberate twofold policy. First, the government sponsored regular large-scale distributions of bread and other foodstuffs to the poor. By the late first century A.D., as many as 150,000 urban Romans received such handouts at hundreds of distribution centers located across the capital city. Second, senators, military generals, and emperors spent huge sums subsidizing public festivals, shows, and games. This policy of appeasing the masses through free food and entertainment eventually became known as *panem et circenses*, or "bread and circuses." For reference, modern scholars often quote a famous sarcastic and bitter remark by the humorist Juvenal (Decimus Junius Juvenalis, ca. A.D.60–ca. 130). "There's only two things that concern the commoners," he said, "bread and [circus] games."[9] Less frequently cited but more informative is this similar statement by the second-century A.D. orator Marcus Cornelius Fronto:

> Because of his shrewd understanding of political science, the emperor [Trajan, reigned 98–117] gave his attention even

Controlling the Commoners

Here, from her *As the Romans Did: A Sourcebook in Roman Social History*, scholar Jo-Ann Shelton elaborates on the means of "crowd control" employed by Roman leaders in the late Republic before the construction of huge facilities for public games.

"The upper class had various methods of keeping the lower classes under control. It could, through senatorial decrees, prohibit or closely regulate gatherings of lower-class people. . . . A more subtle method of manipulating the lower classes was to promote a concept of the ideal Roman as someone who was dutiful (*pius*), hard-working, and serious-minded. The upper class claimed that it was preserving ancestral customs, and it concealed its resistance to political power for the masses by appealing to traditional procedures and virtues. Of course, to an aristocrat who had been brought up to assume a paternalistic [fatherly] attitude toward the lower classes and to think that the masses were incapable of governing themselves, public gatherings and moral decline may well have seemed the same thing. Compare the upper-class promotion of the traditional Roman as a rugged farmer, willing to fight to defend the land he owned; at a time when few families owned land, this image continued to be fostered by wealthy property owners as a kind of proof that they were the conservators of ancestral custom and were thus the proper authorities in the state."

to actors and other performers on stage or on the race track or in the arena, since he knew that the Roman people are held in control principally by two things—free grain and shows—that political support depends as much on the entertainments as on matters of serious import, that neglect of serious problems does the greater harm, but neglect of entertainments brings damaging unpopularity, that gifts [from the emperor] are less eagerly and ardently longed for than shows, and finally, that gifts placate [appease] only the common people on the grain dole, singly and individually, but the shows placate everyone.[10]

Another important way that the games helped to maintain public order and government control in imperial times was by acting as a sort of safety valve for the people's hostility or dissent. It became customary for people with legitimate grievances to approach the emperor at the circus or amphitheater (arena); those leaders who listened respectfully and offered at least some minimal favorable response maintained their popularity, at least for the moment. As explained by Alan Cameron, a noted authority on Roman circus games:

> Provided that it did not get out of hand (and in the early Empire there were normally police provisions adequate to ensure that it did not), even a hostile demonstration could ease a difficult situation. A grievance aired, even if fruitlessly, is a grievance halved. Imagine the tension the first time Nero entered the theater after the murder of [his mother] Agrippina. A joke against him . . . if tolerated, could help to diffuse indignation that, if suppressed, might have smoldered and grown to explode in a much more dangerous way. . . . The games themselves could serve as a

safety valve. Genuine grievances (about a tax, a corn shortage, a minister) would tend to be dissipated in the excitement and resentments of the races. . . . There can be little doubt that, not least among their functions, the games did indeed divert popular attention from what, for most, were the grim and tedious realities of everyday life in Rome.[11]

The *Ludi*

The games that both pleased and placated Roman audiences can be conveniently grouped into two general categories—those that were publicly funded from the start and those that were at first privately funded and much later came to be paid for by the state. Both kinds of games had religious origins. The first category consisted of the *ludi*, which translates variously as "games," "sports," or "plays." These were connected with various religious festivals, the *feriae*, in which people prayed and sacrificed to the gods and then followed up with feasts and sometimes sports contests or exhibitions.

One of the most popular of the *feriae* was the Ludi Romani, a large fifteen-day-long festival held each September to honor Jupiter (the Roman equivalent of the Greek god Zeus, leader of the gods) and two other gods, Juno and Minerva. At least by the third century B.C., the Ludi Romani featured three main varieties of *ludi*—chariot racing (*ludi circenses*); theatrical performances (*ludi scaenici*), including comedies, tragedies, farces, pantomimes, and so on; and wild animal shows (*venationes*).[12]

By late republican times, the *ludi* had also come to be associated with secular (nonreligious) celebrations, notably those following military victories. Before going into battle, for example, a general might pray for Jupiter's support; if victory was achieved, the god received thanksgiving in the form of public games (in this case, referred to as *ludi magni*) held directly following the general's triumphal victory parade. In time, these occasional games became disassociated from the triumph and were celebrated more regularly, frequently during the holidays associated with some of the traditional *feriae* (though these spectacles had no direct religious connection).

Jupiter, chief god of the Roman pantheon, to whom the Ludi Romani festival was dedicated.

Evolution of Roman Chariot Racing

The general trend in which *ludi* started out with strong religious connections and ended up as largely secular events is well illustrated by the evolution of the *ludi circenses*. The Greeks and Etruscans, from whom the Romans borrowed the event, were racing chariots at least as early as the 700s B.C. (and probably earlier, as suggested by descriptions of such races in the *Iliad*, the famous epic poem about the Trojan War by the Greek bard Homer). For both Greeks and Etruscans, who had splendid cities in Italy when Rome was still a backward little town, such races were always part of religious festivals; the same was true of early Roman races. According to a later Roman story, shortly after establishing Rome in 753 B.C., the legendary Romulus held chariot races to help celebrate a harvest thanksgiving, the Consualia (honoring the god Consus, an early agrarian deity, or perhaps a god of the underworld). During these races, the story goes, Romulus and the other Roman men, who had no women with whom to mate and populate the new city, kidnapped the women of the Sabines, a neighboring people who had been invited to the festival.

Whether or not it was Romulus who held the first Roman chariot races (or for that mat-

This first-century A.D. terracotta plaque shows a quadrigarum, *a four-horse chariot, speeding toward the turning posts at the end of the racetrack's* euripus.

ter whether he was even a real person), it is almost certain that such races were for a long time small, infrequent affairs. It took several more centuries for racing to develop into a large-scale institution in Rome. During these centuries, as the Consualia declined in importance and some of its traditions faded and were lost, the religious aspect of the races became increasingly less significant. Finally, by the last few centuries of the Republic, chariot races were viewed mainly as popular secular entertainment.

More Holidays Added

Indeed, the *ludi* became so popular that over time the holidays with which they were associated were extended. The Ludi Cereales (dedicated to Ceres, goddess of grain), for instance, which had originally lasted one day, became a seven-day affair. By the start of the first century B.C., the Romans observed fifty-seven days of *ludi*, grouped into six separate celebrations.[13]

Not surprisingly, staging so many public shows was an extremely expensive proposition for the government, especially considering that admission to the *ludi* was free. As University of California scholar Jo-Ann Shelton explains,

> At the beginning of each year, the Senate would decide how much money it wished to allocate for the *ludi* of each holiday. The production of the *ludi*, however, was entrusted [in republican times] to the aediles [officials who supervised public buildings, markets, and entertainment] (or, in the imperial period, to the praetors [administrators of justice]). It was their job to hire the performers, buy wild animals, purchase necessary equipment, and so on. The senatorial allotment was intended to cover all these expenses, but most of the aediles added to this allotment large amounts of their own money because they hoped to win popularity with the voters by arranging "the greatest show on earth."[14]

Julius Caesar was perhaps the best known of the ambitious republican politicians who attempted to buy popular support through subsidizing public games. As aedile in 65 B.C., he outdid himself in the job, spending large sums of his own money, thereby making himself a household name and significantly contributing to his election as praetor in 63. Later, when he came to wield a great deal more power in Rome, Caesar also increased the annual number of public holidays to seventy-six. And a few years later, his adopted son, Augustus, added another fifteen. (In fact, Augustus sponsored so many races, gladiatorial fights, and other shows, he set a precedent that all of his successors had no choice but to follow if they wanted to keep the urban mob's allegiance.)

Origins of Gladiatorial Combats

The other category of games, which was originally privately funded, was the *munera* (singular, *munus*), mainly spectacles involving gladiators. Along with a number of other customs and ideas, the Romans borrowed gladiatorial combats from the Etruscans. The Etruscans believed that when an important man died, his spirit required a blood sacrifice to survive in the afterlife (hence the literal translation of *munera:* "offerings" or "obligations" to the dead); so outside these individuals' tombs they staged rituals in which warriors fought to the death. In Rome, the *munera* were at first private affairs staged by aristocrats (or at least the wealthy).

Over time, however, both the upper classes and the general populace came to view these combats more as entertainment than as funeral ritual. And demand grew for staging bigger and more exciting gladiatorial shows for public consumption. Julius Caesar was the first leader to stage large-scale *munera*, paid for out of his own pocket when he was aedile in 65 B.C. Plutarch reported that at that time he presented 320 pairs of gladiators,[15] while according to Plutarch's contemporary the Roman historian Suetonius (Gaius Suetonius Tranquillus, ca. A.D. 69–ca. 140):

> Caesar put on a gladiatorial show, but had collected so immense a troop of combatants that his terrified political opponents [fearing that the gladiators might rebel, as had occurred in the uprising led by the gladiator Spartacus a few years before, or that Caesar might use these warriors to stage a government coup] rushed a bill through the [legislature], limiting the number of gladiators that anyone might keep in Rome; consequently far fewer pairs fought than had been advertised.[16]

It was Caesar who also provided a bridge from the older system of training, managing, and paying for gladiators to the one that prevailed in the Empire. Before his time, a well-to-do individual who wanted to put on a gladiatorial show went to a professional supplier called a *lanista*, who procured and trained the fighters. Desiring to give the state more control over these fights, Caesar built a gladiator school (*ludus*) run by senators and other prestigious Romans. The first state-funded public *munera* were held in 44 B.C., just before Caesar's assassination, and in 42, when the aediles created a sensation by substituting gladiatorial bouts for chariot races on a public program. Following these leads, Augustus and the other early emperors soon made staging the *munera* virtually an imperial monopoly. State control and promotion of the games was a crucial factor in the rapid transformation of the "bread and circuses" policy into an ingrained institution.

Julius Caesar, the first Roman leader to stage large-scale arena games.

The Games' Powerful Allure

By the early Empire, the more physical and violent kinds of public shows had become by far Rome's most popular form of entertainment. These included chariot racing, gladiatorial combats, wild beast hunts, and the "combat sport" of boxing (which was staged separately and more informally, since it was not a formal part of either the *ludi* or *munera*). All other kinds of entertainment, including theatrical shows, had much smaller followings.

Evidence for the growing allure of the more violent, or at least more spectacular, shows can be found as early as the second century B.C. The famous Roman playwright Terence (Publius Terentius Afer, ca. 185–ca. 159 B.C.) witnessed, to his dismay, how audiences had begun to express a decided preference for such shows over mere stage plays. Both his first and second attempts to stage his play *The Mother-in-Law* (in 165 B.C. and five years later) failed when the audiences rushed away to see what they viewed as more exciting shows. In the surviving prologue of the play, written for the third attempt to produce it (which succeeded), Terence recaps what happened before and implores the spectators to stay the course this time. (The speech was originally given by Lucius Ambivius Turpio, Terence's producer and leading actor.)

> Now for my sake give a fair hearing to my plea. Once more I am presenting *The Mother-in-Law*, a play for which I have never been able to gain a hearing uninterrupted, so much as misfortune dogged its progress. You can remedy this by your understanding, if you will support our efforts. At the first production, much talk of some boxers, as well as the rumor that a tight-rope walker would appear, the mob of their supporters, shouting, and women's screaming forced me off the stage before the end. I then decided to . . . put it on a second time. The first part was doing well when news arrived that there was to be a gladiators' show. In surged the people, pushing, shouting, jostling for a place, leaving me powerless to hold my own. Today there is no distraction, all is calm and peaceful; this is my chance to present the play and your opportunity to do honor to the stage. Do not be responsible for allowing the art of drama to sink into the hands of a few. . . . Grant my plea on behalf of the author. . . . Do not let him be cheated and derided by unjust men. For my sake . . . listen in silence. Others will then feel encouraged to write [plays], and it will be profitable for me in the future to present new plays bought at my own expense.[17]

In a way, this plea ultimately fell on deaf ears. In the century or so that followed, Roman drama did "sink," as audiences increasingly came to prefer and demand more spectacular forms of entertainment. Compared to large-scale chariot races and fights to the death among gladiators and wild animals, traditional plays like Terence's seemed tame; by the early years of the Empire, the demand for plays with careful plotting, dialogue, and characterization had all but disappeared.[18] In the realm of entertainment, public tastes were now shaped mainly by the powerful allure of the great public spectacles, a situation that would endure for centuries to come.

CHAPTER 2

Rome's Monumental Games Facilities

The huge size and grandeur of the public facilities that housed the Roman games reflected the fact that the Romans were great builders—overall the most prolific, efficient, and practical in the ancient world. Indeed, as the late, noted classical scholar Edith Hamilton pointed out, the true Roman artist was not the painter, sculptor, or poet, but the engineer. "Roman genius was called into action by the enormous practical needs of a world empire,"[19] she wrote. And Rome met these needs appropriately and magnificently by producing a vast network of roads for the swift transport of armies and trade goods; miles of aqueducts that supplied life-giving water to sustain hundreds of cities and towns; as well as great circuses for chariot racing and amphitheaters where gladiators and beasts fought and died.

This artist's rendition of part of the Roman Forum during the second century A.D. illustrates the Romans' mastery of monumental architecture.

The Romans did not invent roads, aqueducts, and games facilities, of course. As with the public games themselves, they borrowed many of the architectural ideas and construction techniques for the games facilities and other buildings from the Etruscans and Greeks. (The arch, for example, which the Romans used repeatedly in their amphitheaters, theaters, aqueducts, and numerous other structures, and which became one of their trademarks, originated with the Etruscans.) And as the Roman games eventually became larger in scope than any seen before, so too did the games facilities. The size, durability, and sheer numbers of racetracks, like Rome's mammoth Circus Maximus, and amphitheaters, like the imposing Colosseum, also in the capital city, far surpassed any entertainment facilities built anywhere in the world up till that time.

On the one hand, these enormous structures were practical. Considering that the public games became Rome's most popular form of entertainment, they had to be very large to accommodate the great crowds that desired to attend. Yet at the same time, these facilities transcended practicality, becoming, by virtue of their great size and splendor, symbols of Roman power and cultural achievement.

Early Makeshift Arenas

Not surprisingly, large stone amphitheaters (*amphitheatri*) like the renowned Colosseum (built in the 70s and early 80s A.D.) did not appear overnight; rather, they evolved gradually from smaller, less durable, and less impressive structures, as demanded by the ongoing growth in the size and popularity of the games. The first permanent Roman amphitheaters were built in the first century B.C., the tumultuous period in which the Republic endured numerous crises and finally collapsed, giving way to the Empire. But long before this time, small-scale gladiatorial bouts and other shows were held on an occasional but semiregular basis. Because these events attracted considerable crowds, they were staged in wide, open areas, most often the forums (main squares) of cities. We know this because of a reference made by the Roman architect and engineer Vitruvius (Marcus Vitruvius Pollio, first century B.C.) in his *De architectura (On Architecture)*: "The custom of giving gladiatorial shows in the forum has been handed down from our ancestors."[20]

Eventually, the Romans began building wooden arenas to accommodate public shows. It is likely that the first such structures consisted mainly of consecutive rows of seats set up in or around the forums where the games took place; however, in time these makeshift facilities became separate, freestanding buildings in their own right. Some were dismantled and reassembled as need dictated. Others may have stood intact for several seasons before being demolished to make way for houses, temples, or other structures.

Though impermanent, these early arenas were often very large and elaborate, featuring seating for thousands or even tens of thousands of people. To build a typical facility of this type required huge amounts of wood and nails and the labor of hundreds of builders and other craftsmen. This made the construction of such an arena, like the often elaborate games presented within it, an extremely expensive proposition that only wealthy aristocrats and businessmen could afford. Yet erecting stone amphitheaters was considerably *more* time-consuming and expensive, so even after the first stone versions appeared, people continued to supplement them with wooden ones.

The ruins of the Colosseum, Rome's greatest and most famous amphitheater.

Luckily, most of the individuals who financed wooden amphitheaters were responsible enough to hire skilled architects and builders to ensure proper design and construction. But now and then, less reputable speculators trying to turn a fast profit hastily threw up structures that were poorly designed or built with substandard materials. Such shady practices occasionally led to disaster. In his *Annals*, Tacitus recorded the following gripping account of the collapse of a wooden arena in Fidenae, a town just north of Rome, in A.D. 27:

> An ex-slave called Atilius started building an amphitheater at Fidenae for a gladiatorial show. But he neither rested its foundations on solid ground nor fastened the wooden superstructure securely. He had undertaken the project not because of great wealth or municipal ambition but for sordid profits. Lovers of such displays . . . flocked in—men and women of all ages. Their numbers, swollen by the town's proximity, intensified the tragedy. The packed structure collapsed, subsiding both inwards and outwards and . . . overwhelming a huge crowd of spectators and bystanders. Those killed at the outset of the catastrophe at least escaped torture. . . . More pitiable were those, mangled but not yet dead, who knew their wives and children lay there too. In daytime they could see them, and at night they heard their screams and moans. . . . When the ruins began to be cleared, people rushed to embrace and kiss the corpses—and even quarreled over them, when features were unrecognizable but similarities of physique and age had caused wrong identifications. Fifty thousand people were mutilated or crushed in the disaster.[21]

Judging that the tragedy was the result of cutting corners because of inadequate funds, the Roman Senate decreed that henceforth no entrepreneur with less than 400,000 sesterces (a very large sum at the time) could attempt such a project.

The First Stone Amphitheaters

Stone amphitheaters were much sturdier, safer, and of course more durable and permanent. The first all-stone version in Italy was erected about the year 80 B.C. in the small city of Pompeii, located on what is now the Bay of Naples, about 140 miles southeast of Rome. Because the now famous A.D. 79 volcanic eruption of nearby Mount Vesuvius encased the town in a protective layer of ash, the amphitheater is well preserved. In fact, the inscription carved to dedicate the building still survives, bearing the names of the two prominent public officials who constructed it—Valgus and Porcius. Because the Latin term *amphitheatrum* had not yet been coined, the inscription refers to the structure as a *spectaculum*, or a "place for spectacles."

The amphitheater at Pompeii, pictured here, was preserved under a layer of volcanic ash.

Also still plainly visible are the design details of the oval facility, which measures 445 by 341 feet and originally sat some twenty thousand people, roughly Pompeii's entire population. The arena floor, where the shows took place, is sunken below the level of the outside ground, so an earthen embankment helps support the great weight of many of the rising tiers of stone seats. Providing support for the stadium's curved walls is an outer perimeter of high brick arches and several large exterior staircases.

Despite their excellent state of preservation, the Pompeiian amphitheater's bare stones offer only a fragmentary impression of what the building was like in its glory. No longer visible are the many comforts and amenities the crowds of spectators enjoyed. Among these were elegant decorations such as statues and tapestries; cushions to sit on; fast-food stands surrounding the complex, and perhaps roving vendors selling refreshments in the stands; and a huge awning, or *velarium*, that shaded the audience on hot sunny days. That the awning above could be nearly as important to a spectator's enjoyment as the shows staged below is evidenced by an advertisement that the volcanic ash preserved on a city wall: "The gladiatorial troop hired by Aulus Suettius Certus will fight in Pompeii on May 31. There will also be a wild animal hunt. The awnings will be used."[22]

Because of the great expense of building and maintaining stone amphitheaters, for a long time few towns attempted to match Pompeii's achievement.[23] Even in Rome, the capital of what was then the most powerful and prosperous empire in world history, building a properly grand stone amphitheater remained an elusive goal. In 29 B.C., fully half a century after the dedication of the Pompeiian arena, T. Statilius Taurus, one of Octavian's generals, constructed an

Amphitheaters in Italy and the Provinces

In the three centuries or so following the creation of the Pompeiian amphitheater, the first constructed entirely of stone masonry, the Romans built dozens of similar arenas throughout Italy and across the Empire. In addition to the largest and most famous—the Colosseum in Rome—these included the huge amphitheater at Capua, about 110 miles southeast of the capital, which measured 560 by 460 feet and stood 95 feet high; the arena at Puteoli (modern Pozzuoli), across the Bay of Naples from Pompeii, measuring 490 by 370 feet; northern Italy's impressive Verona amphitheater, with dimensions of 500 by 405 feet and a seating capacity of 25,000 to 28,000; and similarly large versions at Nimes and Arles, both in Gaul (what is now France), and at Thysdrus, in northern Africa.

Many towns had smaller, but no less beautiful and sturdy, arenas. Typical was the amphitheater at Trier, originally called *Augusta Treverorum*, a prosperous town on the Moselle River in northeastern Gaul. The masonry structure went up sometime in the early second century A.D., probably on the site where wooden versions had stood for some time. The amphitheater's bowl was about 230 feet long and accommodated approximately seven thousand people. The vast majority of such structures were built from scratch as oval-shaped masonry shells with dirt arenas, also oval shaped, in their centers. However, a few, such as the arenas at Dodona, in western Greece, and Xanthos, in Asia Minor (what is now Turkey), had been Greek theaters, which had presented plays, before the Romans converted them to accommodate gladiator fights and wild beast shows.

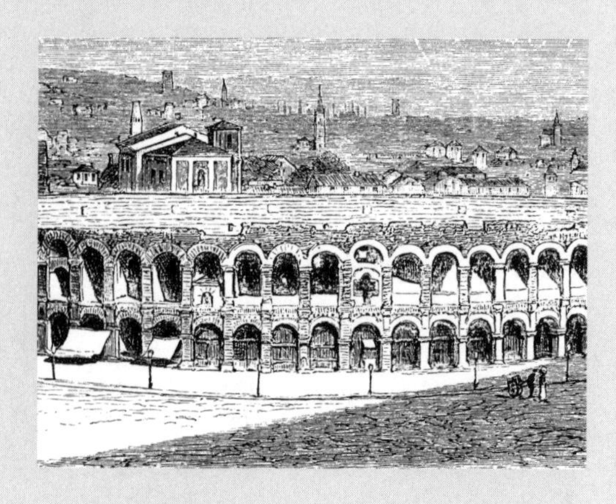

The Roman amphitheater at Verona (in northern Italy) is one of the many such structures still partially preserved.

amphitheater in Rome's Campus Martius (a large open area near the Tiber River). Because this arena no longer exists, historians are uncertain about its seating capacity. But it was surely far too small to satisfy the needs of a city the size of Rome, which by this time had a population of perhaps nearly a million. Another drawback was that, to save expense, Taurus's builders used both wood and stone, leaving the building seriously prone to damage by fire, which in fact eventually destroyed it.

A Pressing Need for a New Amphitheater

During the roughly nine decades in which Taurus's stadium remained intact, the early emperors evidently felt that it, supplemented by the temporary wooden versions erected from time to time, was enough to serve the capital. About the year A.D. 57, for example, Nero built a wooden amphitheater. According to Suetonius, the arena rose in the Campus Martius and took "less than a year" to build.[24] But eventually the seating capacities of this and Taurus's arena proved inadequate, and increasingly various games and shows normally staged in amphitheaters had to be held in the Circus Maximus, the city's large elliptical horse-racing facility. Clearly, there was a pressing need in Rome for a permanent amphitheater of the Colosseum's size and caliber.

The chain of events leading to the Colosseum's construction began in A.D. 64, when a terrible fire devastated about two-thirds of Rome. The blaze began in the wooden seats of the Circus Maximus, raged for nine days, and destroyed thousands of homes, temples, and public buildings, including Taurus's amphitheater. To his credit, Nero organized shelters for the homeless and launched ambitious rebuilding projects. (The old adage about his starting the fire and reciting poetry while watching the city burn is almost certainly false.) In the process, he realigned many formerly winding streets on an efficient grid pattern and introduced a strict new building code that greatly reduced the risk of fires.

However, Nero devoted a larger portion of the state treasury to building projects that benefited him alone. One immense area the great fire had cleared, comprising nearly 350 acres of prime real estate in the heart of the city, had room for dozens of public buildings, including perhaps a new and properly spectacular amphitheater. But Nero, a conceited and self-indulgent individual, decided to transform the entire area into his own personal pleasure park and palace. Under the direction of his talented architect, Severus, and chief engineer, Celer, what became known as the *Domus Aurea,* or Golden House, rose from the rubble left by the great fire. The grandiose project was essentially a wealthy country villa set in the middle of the world's most crowded urban center. "The entrance-hall," wrote Suetonius, "was large enough to contain a huge statue of himself [Nero], 120 feet high."[25]

Though Nero did not realize it at the time, his decadent days were numbered and his magnificent new palace was marked for a new round of large-scale urban renewal. In

A fanciful depiction of Nero persecuting the early Christians for supposedly starting the great fire of A.D. 64.

Nero's Golden House

In his *Lives of the Twelve Caesars,* Suetonius provides this description of the palatial residence and parklands Nero built after the great fire ravaged the capital city, a project the ancient historian sarcastically termed the emperor's "monument to himself":

"An enormous pool, like a sea, was surrounded by buildings made to resemble cities, and by a landscape garden consisting of plowed fields, vineyards, pastures, and woodlands—where every variety of domestic and wild animal roamed about. Parts of the house were overlaid with gold [giving the place its name] and studded with precious stones and mother-of-pearl. All the dining-rooms had ceilings of . . . ivory, the panels of which could slide back and let a rain of flowers, or of perfume from hidden sprinklers, shower upon his guests. The main dining room was circular, and its roof revolved, day and night, in time with the sky. Sea water, or sulfur water, was always on tap in the baths. When the palace had been decorated throughout in this lavish style, Nero dedicated it, and condescended to remark, 'Good, now I can at last begin to live like a human being!'"

Nero's successors leveled his Golden House, but a few of its basement vaults, including the one pictured here, survived.

June 68, having been branded an enemy of the people by the Senate, he committed suicide. And in a conscious effort to bury the memory of his reign, his immediate successors decided to construct a magnificent new amphitheater in the middle of his pleasure park. Thus, ironically, from the wreckage of the colossal and impermanent symbol of one Roman's monstrous vanity emerged the mighty Colosseum, which would turn out to be an eternal symbol of all the Romans as a great people.

The Colosseum's Dimensions and Features

The facility's original name was the *Amphitheatrum Flavium,* or "Amphitheater of the Flavians." This referred to the fact that the emperor Vespasian (reigned 69–79), who began its construction, and his sons Titus (79–81) and Domitian (81–96), who completed it, were members of the noble Flavian family line. Not until early medieval times, well after the Roman Empire had disintegrated, did the name "Colosseum" come into general use.[26] Most of the structure's main features were completed by the summer of 80, during Titus's reign; the finishing touches were added after his untimely death in September of the following year, when his brother ascended the throne.

In its original majesty, the building's oval bowl measured 620 by 513 feet in breadth and over 156 feet in height. The oval arena floor, outlined by and butting up against a protective wall at the bottom of the seating section *(cavea),* was 287 feet long by 180 feet wide. Because the structure's seating sections no longer exist, the exact seating capacity is unknown, but most historians agree on an estimate of about fifty thousand. The *cavea* was divided into five separate zones, called *maeniana*, each designated for specific persons or classes of people. The first *maenianum* consisted of the *podium*, a spacious marble terrace that ran around the upper edges of the protective wall, an area reserved for high-ranking or sacred personages such as the *pontifex maximus*, head priest of the state religion, and the Vestal Virgins, priestesses of Vesta (goddess of the hearth). On the north side of this platform was the *pulvinar*, or royal box, in which the emperor and his family sat. Opposite this, on the south side of the *podium*, was a box reserved for the prefect of the city, the public official who oversaw the day-to-day operation of Rome's public works and institutions.

Rising above the *podium* were the other zones: the second, a tier of seats reserved for senators and other distinguished private citizens; the third, for members of the middle class; the fourth, for slaves and foreigners;

The remains of the Colosseum's pulvinar, *or royal box, are visible behind a modern railing.*

A cutaway view of the Colosseum reveals the gangways circling the arena. The arched passage on the bottom level opened into several exits.

and the fifth, the *maenianum summum*, consisting of wooden seating installed under a roofed colonnade (row of columns) at the very top of the building, for women. The custom of making women sit farthest away from the arena floor may have originated with Augustus's edict to that effect, designed to shelter women from seeing (and presumably being disturbed at the sight of) the blood and brutality of the spectacles. The very poorest Romans, who had no money to purchase regular seats, were allowed to stand behind the women's bleachers.

Although not a permanent feature of stone or wood, the *velarium*, the giant awning that sometimes covered the amphitheater's open top, was as important to the spectators as their seats. They typically sat watching the games and spectacles for many hours at a stretch. Without protection from the hot Mediterranean sun, this would have resulted in much discomfort, as well as painful sunburns.

The highly specialized work of raising, lowering, and maintaining the awning was entrusted to sailors stationed at Misenum, a naval port on the western Italian coast south of Rome. About a hundred of these men lived in barracks near the amphitheater, and at least a couple times a year several hundred more arrived from Misenum to help them. They raised and lowered the great canopy using an ingenious system of ropes, pulleys, and winches. The ropes, which ran over poles jutting from the top of the fourth level to winches

An artist's conception of the complex array of ropes, pulleys, and winches used to raise and lower the Colosseum's awning (velarium).

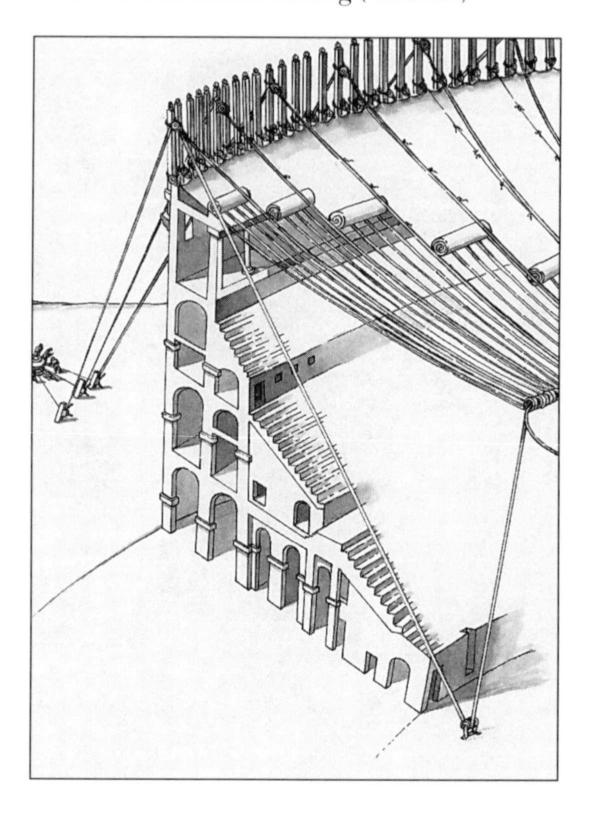

located outside the building, formed a spider's weblike lattice across the arena. The lattice held up the individual canvas strips that, when lowered into place one beside another, combined to form the full *velarium*.

As the amphitheater's official aerial riggers, these sailors must also have been charged with creating various "special effects" ordered from time to time by the emperor or by the magistrate who organized the spectacles. For instance, the first-century A.D. poet Publius Papinius Statius, who enjoyed Domitian's patronage, described "the line." This was evidently a rope (or network of ropes) slung across the top of the arena, from which fruit, nuts, and other treats showered down on the delighted spectators. "Scarce was the new dawn stirring," Statius recalled in his *Silvae*,

> when already sweetmeats were raining from the line . . . the famous fruit of Pontic nut-groves, or of Idume's [Palestine's] fertile slopes [probably dates, for which Palestine was famous]. . . . Biscuits and melting pastries, Amerian fruit [apples and pears] not over-ripe, must-cakes, and bursting dates from invisible palms were showering down. . . . Let Jupiter send his tempests through the world and threaten the broad fields, while our own Jove [another name for Jupiter, in this case a reference to the emperor] sends us showers like these.[27]

Raising the Colosseum's Awning

In this excerpt from his book, *Rome of the Caesars,* Italian scholar Leonardo B. Dal Maso tells how the sailors from the Roman port of Misenum operated the complex rigging and machinery that moved the Colosseum's huge awning.

"The whole apparatus centered on the great ring, like a sort of skylight, to which the ropes holding up the canopy were attached. In the first phase, the ring was raised from the arena [floor level] as far as the level of the cornice [the horizontal roof of the top circular colonnade]: this operation was carried out with ropes which went from the ring to the pulleys at the top of the poles [standing upright on the building's upper perimeter] and from the pulleys to the outside . . . being attached to the 160 large blocks of stone surrounding the amphitheater below. On each of these blocks there was a winch . . . with pulleys for rolling up the ropes. The 160 winches were turned in perfect unison to the beating of time, and this is what raised the ring. When the ring was raised, the ends of the ropes were pulled up and tied to the poles. In the second phase, a second rope was lowered from each of the poles and attached to the ring at a level lower than the first rope: this lower series of ropes, tightened by other pulleys and winches on the terrace of the top gallery . . . formed a sort of spider's web which held up the canvases of the *velarium*. These converging sections were unrolled from above, tied to each other, until they reached the central ring. . . . If all these requirements are taken into account, along with the enormous surface of the *velarium*, the huge weight of the ropes . . . and the static and dynamic problems created by resistance and tension, it must be concluded that raising the canopy was a much more difficult undertaking than erecting an obelisk [a tall, pointed stone structure of enormous weight]."

The Colosseum Inaugurated

Since the Colosseum's main structural features—its entrances, stone seating, and arena floor—had been completed by the summer of the year 80, Titus went ahead and inaugurated the building. (The principal motive for his haste was probably public relations. Earlier that year a serious fire had damaged several sections of the city, and cheering up the despondent populace by holding lavish games was a sure way to boost his popularity.)

These inaugural games, among the most famous (or infamous?) in Roman history, lasted for one hundred days and were extremely elaborate and costly. Unfortunately, no detailed day-to-day account of them has survived; however, fragmentary descriptions by Suetonius, Dio Cassius (ca. 163–ca. 235), and other ancient historians give a general idea of the large scale and diversity of the events staged in the new arena. Apparently, more than nine thousand animals of various kinds were slaughtered during the fourteen weeks the games lasted, five thousand of these in a single day. Thousands of gladiators fought and hundreds of condemned criminals met their deaths by either gladiators' swords or the claws of beasts. As the following account by Dio Cassius informs us, animals fought animals, men (and also women) fought animals, and ships fought ships.

Titus, the second Flavian emperor, succeeded his father, Vespasian, in A.D. *79.*

> There was a battle between cranes and also between four elephants; animals both tame and wild were slain. . . . And women (not those of any prominence, however) took part in dispatching them. As for men, several fought in single combat and several groups contended together both in infantry and naval battles. For Titus suddenly filled this same theater with water and brought in horses and bulls and some other domesticated animals that had been taught to behave in the liquid element just as on land. He also brought in people on ships, who engaged in a sea-fight there.[28]

Titus's inaugural festivities were only the beginning of a long tradition of spectacles—some of them colorful and exciting, others brutal and frightening—that the Colosseum and other Roman amphitheaters would host in ensuing centuries. Many emperors and local magistrates would strive mightily to outdo their predecessors. And some would succeed.

A modern rendering of animals and humans fighting for their lives in the Colosseum. Over the centuries, perhaps millions of animals met violent ends in Roman amphitheaters.

The Development of Circuses

Like the amphitheater, the other major kind of Roman games facility, the circus, was originally an informal, impermanent arrangement that gradually developed into a formal, permanent structure with characteristic features. "When circuses first appeared on Italian soil," explains John H. Humphrey, an expert on Roman circuses,

> it was not in their fully evolved form as we know it from the later Empire: the evolution towards that final, highly elaborate and highly successful form, was a slow one, and . . . only achieved what we would now recognize as the "typical" aspect of a Roman circus by about the early years of the second century A.D. Whereas . . . the amphitheater [in its wooden form] became established in Campanian [west-central Italian] cities during the second century B.C., the circus, although in existence in Rome from the time of the Kings, only became a fully integrated architectural form probably as a result of the work on the Circus Maximus by Caesar and Augustus [in the late first century B.C.], work which was taken to its logical conclusion by [the emperor] Trajan in the years immediately following his accession [to the throne] in A.D. 98. In short, circuses in their canonical [final, fixed] and monumental form were a later architectural development than . . . amphitheaters, despite the fact that Rome possessed what was called a circus as early as the . . . sixth century B.C.[29]

The reason for this apparent contradiction is that the first Roman circuses were makeshift affairs, similar to the Etruscan and Greek versions on which they were based. The Greeks raced horses and chariots in hippodromes. These were essentially flat and relatively stone-free open areas in which people set up temporary wooden starting gates and turning posts. Some also featured banks of earth piled up along the sides for spectators to stand on for a better view. Etruscan sports arenas, which apparently housed both equestrian and athletic events, were also makeshift and impermanent, although more elaborate than Greek hippodromes. Paintings of such arenas in tombs and on vases suggest that they had wooden bleachers on at least two sides and tall vertical posts that held overhead awnings.[30]

The earliest Roman circuses were probably little more than flat open areas with temporary turning posts and banks of earth, like Greek hippodromes. It is unknown when the first Etruscan-style wooden bleachers were added, but this development may date to the erection of the first version of the Circus Maximus, in the valley between Rome's Palatine and Aventine hills, about 600 B.C. According to the Roman historian Livy (Titus Livius, 59 B.C.–A.D. 17), King Tarquin (Tarquinius Priscus)

> celebrated public games on a scale more elaborate and opulent than any of his predecessors. It was on this occasion that our Circus Maximus was originally planned. On the ground marked out for it special places were assigned to Senators and knights to erect their stands in—or "decks" as they were called. These stands were supported on props and raised twelve feet from the ground. Horses and boxers . . . provided the entertainment. From then onward the games became an annual institution.[31]

A Wonder of the World

In the centuries that followed, the Circus Maximus underwent occasional but continuous elaboration and improvement. According to Humphrey, the starting gates (*carceres*) were added in 329 B.C. And shortly before his assassination in 44 B.C., Julius Caesar undertook a major renovation of the structure. Still, in his day at least three-quarters of the seating section was still made of wood (the fewer stone seats being reserved for senators and other important citizens). Not surprisingly, this presented a fire hazard, and indeed, several fires (in addition to the one in A.D. 64) ravaged the facility, one of the worst in 31 B.C. (prompting a new renovation by Augustus). Not until Trajan's renovation, in the early second century A.D., did all of the Circus Maximus's seating become stone.

The Circus Maximus in its prime, from Trajan's time until the fifth century (a period in which later emperors continued to improve it), must surely have been one of the wonders of the world.[32] University of Louisville scholar Robert B. Kebric provides the following description of the structure at the height of its glory.

> The Circus was immense by any standard. Externally, its length was about 680 yards (over a third of a mile), while its width was 150 yards. The most recent estimates place its seating capacity at about 150,000, although some ancient sources make it 250,000 and more. It is difficult to reconcile this discrepancy. . . . The Romans were notorious for overcrowd-

ing, and we can never know how many people they actually packed into the Circus. . . . The ancient figures may have included those who watched from the hills overlooking the track. . . . The arena of the Circus measured about 635 by 85 yards, or roughly twelve times that of the Colosseum, another of Rome's great spectator facilities. Its floor was a bed of compacted earth covered with a layer of sand, designed to allow the chariots to hold the track (especially on the turns), to save the horses from injury, and to drain off water. . . . At one end of the Circus were twelve starting gates. Running down the middle of the arena, closer to the rounded end of the facility, was a long, narrow barrier (frequently identified as the *spina* but more accurately called the *euripus*). Approximately 365 yards in length, it was covered with an assortment of shrines, altars, and other monuments, including two large obelisks brought from Egypt. It was around this barrier, which had turning posts (*metae*) at each end, that the chariots whirled seven death-defying times (about 3 miles), always to the driver's left.[33]

Today, large sections of this majestic structure remain buried beneath extensive layers of dirt and debris accumulated over the many centuries following Rome's decline. The site occupied by the Circus Maximus has been turned into an archaeological park, and excavation continues; however, the sheer enormity of the job makes it an extremely expensive and slow process that will take perhaps decades more to complete. Indeed, says Humphrey, "No single circus can be completely excavated during the working lifetime of one professional archaeologist if the excavation is going to be conducted according to the standards that are currently acceptable."[34]

For these and other reasons, most of the other Roman circuses built across the Empire in ancient times have been only partially unearthed or remain wholly unexposed and uninvestigated.[35] A few, however, have been substantially excavated and studied, among these the Circus of Maxentius (one of the capital city's four major racetracks, along with the Circus Maximus, Circus Flaminius, and Circus of Caligula and Nero); the circus at Tyre (on the coast of Lebanon); the circus at Mérida in central Spain; and the circus at Lepcis Magna, on the coast of Libya. Together with the imposing remains of the Colosseum and other surviving amphitheaters, these emerging racetracks clearly demonstrate that Roman builders, the finest of antiquity, expended some of their greatest energies on games facilities.

CHAPTER 3

Gladiators: Their Public Image, Lives, and Training

Even today, many centuries after the last gladiators died in Roman amphitheaters, people find these arena warriors fascinating. Reenactments of gladiatorial combats have been featured in modern novels and movies (the most famous in both cases being *Spartacus*), and gladiator-like fights to the death have increasingly become the focus of popular video games (such as "Mortal Kombat"). There are also, of course, a number of modern combat sports, including boxing, judo, karate, and the so-called ultimate fighting. But in none of these is the object to kill one's opponent; serious injuries and death are relatively rare in these sports. Perhaps it is the element of mortal danger involved in the Roman *munera* that many people today find fascinating. The idea of competitors routinely killing one another to entertain the public is so alien to modern cultural and social values that it may evoke a touch of morbid curiosity as well as feelings of disquiet or horror.

For the ancient Romans, by contrast, the gladiatorial fights, including their often lethal outcomes, were a widely accepted form of mass entertainment. And the public images of the gladiators themselves, as well as the way they were treated outside the arena (including their social status, procurement, and training), reflected the Romans' own unique cultural and social values. Clearly, the Romans were a good deal more fascinated by gladiators than are modern audiences, and for reasons peculiar to their own time, place, and traditions.

Crude and Loathsome Characters

First, the Roman fascination for gladiators was bound up in large degree with an obsessive and seemingly contradictory form of hero worship. On the one hand, socially speaking, these warriors were viewed as debased, worthless, and undignified lowlife; like actors and other entertainers, they bore the degrading stigma of *infamia* ("bad reputation"). As the second-century B.C. Latin writer Calpurnius Flaccus put it, "There is no meaner condition among the people than that of the gladiator."[36]

This low status had far-reaching negative implications for gladiators' public image, self-esteem, social opportunities, and their lives in general. People commonly referred to them as crude (*importunus*), indecent (*obscaenus*), damned (*damnatus*), and hopeless (*perditus*). And writers routinely slandered or poked fun at them, often comparing them directly or indirectly to prostitutes, criminals, effeminate actors, and other characters widely seen as unsavory.[37] Many gladiators were bought and sold like cattle, mainly because a majority of them began as slaves or prisoners; and even those that gained their freedom or were free to begin with were seen as little or no better than slaves.

Many gladiators could not escape their degrading social status even in death, for their corpses were not permitted proper burial (unless a relative, friend, or admirer claimed the body and buried it privately). An inscription found at the site of ancient Sarsina (in northeastern Italy) states that three classes of people are not allowed in its new cemetery: suicides by hanging, those involved in immoral trades (i.e., prostitutes, actors, and so on), and gladiators.

Women gladiators were generally viewed as particularly scandalous and loathsome. They were, to be sure, far less numerous and prominent than their male counterparts. But they did come into style briefly from time to time, most notably under the emperor Domitian, who enjoyed watching women fight and paired them against male dwarves as well as against one another. Common adopted or "stage" names for female arena fighters were Achillia (a feminine form of Achilles, the warrior hero of the *Iliad*), and Amazon (a reference to the legendary race of warrior women in Greek mythology). Juvenal, whose satires ridiculed so many diverse aspects of society, was unusually hard on the "gladiatress":

> And what about female athletes, with their purple track-suits, and wrestling in the mud? Not to mention our lady-fencers. We've all seen *them*, stabbing the stump with a foil, shield well advanced, going through the proper motions. Just the right training needed to blow a matronly horn at the Floral Festival [held in late April and early May; all Roman festivals began with trumpet volleys]—unless they have higher ambitions, and the goal of all their practice is the real arena. But then, what modesty can be looked for in some helmeted vixen, a renegade from her sex, who thrives on masculine violence—yet would not prefer to *be* a man, since the pleasure is so much less? What a fine sight for some husband—*it might be you*—his wife's equipment put up at auction, sword-belt, armlet, plumes [helmet decorations], and one odd shin-guard! Or, if the other style of fighting takes her fancy, imagine your delight when the dear girl sells off her greaves [lower leg protectors]! . . . Note how she snorts at each practice thrust, bowed down by the weight of her helmet . . . then wait for the laugh, when she lays down her weapons and squats over the potty![38]

A wall painting found at Pompeii shows gladiators preparing to fight. The man with the curved trumpet is one of several musicians who provided background music for the combats.

On occasion, Roman women, like the one pictured in this mosaic, fought in the arena.

For a woman of slave or lower-class status to become a gladiator was bad enough; but for an upper-class woman to do so was seen as especially revolting and disreputable. According to Tacitus, the ninth year of Nero's reign (A.D. 63) "witnessed gladiatorial displays on a no less magnificent scale than before, but exceeding all precedent in the number of distinguished women and senators disgracing themselves in the arena."[39] Eventually, the emperor Septimus Severus (reigned 193–211) banned female combatants from the arena.

The Model for a Person of Honor

Blatantly and rather oddly contradicting all of this public scorn for and social discrimination against gladiators was the fact that their exploits in the arena were often admired. And those who won often became popular heroes on a par with today's biggest football, baseball, and basketball stars. These fortunate few usually won their freedom (if they began as slaves), enjoyed the applause and sometimes the gifts of fans (including large sums of money and estates given by emperors to a selected few), and could have their pick of beautiful young women (who were the equivalent of the groupies who sometimes attach themselves to modern rock stars). The Roman humorist Martial (Marcus Valerius Martialis, ca. A.D. 40– ca. 104) sang the praises of one such arena hero in one of his popular epigrams:

> Hermes, favorite fighter of the age; Hermes, skilled in all weaponry; Hermes, gladiator and trainer both; Hermes, tempest [storm] and tremor [earthquake] of his school . . . Hermes, taught to win without wounding [i.e., by disarming his opponents] . . . Hermes, darling and distress of gladiators' women [i.e., they either loved him or feared he would kill their men] . . . Hermes, glory of Mars [god of war] universal; Hermes, all things in one and thrice unique.[40]

The reasons for this adulation seem to have been closely related to the Romans' peculiar and conservative ethical notions about the nature of honor and the virtue of submission to authority. In the first place, they perceived in a gladiator's sacrifice of blood a sadly tragic, but still heroic, figure to be admired and honored. The gladiator took a solemn oath that he (or she) would die, unflinchingly and unhesitatingly, for an audience of "betters." Such an act of complete and ultimate submission to the will of one's "master" made the gladiator, in Roman eyes, a model for a person of honor. "Consider the blows they endure!" Cicero exclaimed in a powerfully worded passage.

Consider how they who have been well-disciplined prefer to accept a blow than shamefully avoid it! How often it is made clear that they consider nothing other than the satisfaction of their master or the people! Even when they are covered with wounds they send a messenger to their master to inquire his will. If they have given satisfaction to their masters, they are pleased to fall. What even mediocre gladiator ever groans, ever alters the expression on his face? Which one of them acts shamefully either standing or falling? And which of them, even when he does succumb, ever contracts his neck when ordered to receive the [death] blow?[41]

This view of the gladiator's sacrifice is perhaps not surprising. Recognition of and submission to higher authority was, after all, one of the pillars of the Roman political and patronage systems; it was also a pillar of religion, for the gods represented an authority that even the mightiest human was obliged to obey. Thus, when a gladiator bravely faced and accepted death, he was for an instant transformed into a version of one of Rome's most ideal figures—the soldier who gives his life for the homeland. And, in that brief moment, he and his audience connected with, ennobled, and empowered each other. Lucius Annaeus Seneca (ca. 4 B.C.–A.D. 65), the brilliant and urbane philosopher and playwright who for a time acted as an adviser to Nero, offered this military analogy of a soldier called on by his general (and the state) to shed blood and die if necessary:

> Soldiers glory in their wounds and gladly vaunt themselves over the blood they were privileged to shed; though those who returned from the fray unhurt may have fought as well, the man who brings back a wound is more respected. . . . The recruit pales at the thought of a wound; the veteran can look at his flowing gash with composure, for he knows that he has often won the victory after losing blood. . . .

A Roman mosaic depicts various scenes from a gladiatorial show. On one level, the gladiator symbolized the sacrifice of a soldier dying for his country.

> So God hardens and scrutinizes and exercises those he approves and loves. . . . The most hazardous duties are assigned to the bravest soldiers. . . . And no man in such a detachment will say, "The general has treated me badly," but rather, "The general thinks well of me." Similarly, those told to undergo what cowards and weaklings would weep over should say, "God has judged us fit subjects to test how much human nature can endure."[42]

Another way that gladiatorial fights compared favorably and honorably to the military in the Roman mind was by reenacting, in a sense, legendary battles by warriors of old. Both the Romans and the Greeks harbored a fond nostalgia for the "good old days" (often referred to as the "Age of Heroes"), when the most formidable warriors supposedly faced off in one-on-one duels before their assembled armies, as in Homer's *Iliad*. In a very real way, gladiators' arena exploits recalled the courage and honor of such ancient combats.

Deeply Rooted Traditions and Beliefs

Thus, the Romans maintained a strange societal double standard about gladiators and other arena fighters. Tertullian (Quintus Septimius Tertullianus, ca. 155–ca. 221), a Roman lawyer who converted to and became a great apologist for Christianity, noted this contradictory attitude with unconcealed disdain:

> Men give them [gladiators] their souls, women their bodies too. . . . On one and the same account, they glorify them and degrade and diminish them—indeed, they openly condemn them to ignominy [dishonor and humiliation] and the loss of civil rights, excluding them from the Senate House and rostrum [speaker's platform], the senatorial and equestrian [social] orders, and all other honors or distinctions of any type. The perversity of it! Yet, they love whom they punish; they belittle whom they esteem; the art they glorify, the artist they debase. What judgment is this? On account of that for which he is vilified [condemned], he [the gladiator] is deemed worthy of merit![43]

In addition, there may have been a deeper psychological aspect of the public fascination for gladiators and the violent entertainment they provided. Put another way, this fascination may have constituted the outward expression of emotions, feelings, and beliefs deeply ingrained in Roman culture. Some

A haruspex *(diviner) slaughters a chicken to study the divine "signs" revealed in its internal organs.*

Slaves languish in a Roman slave market. Most gladiators began as slaves, although those who fought well and survived long enough could and often did earn their freedom.

scholars suggest, for example, that the appeal of the bloody arena derived partly from an artifact of Roman religion, namely a superstitious awe of and interest in death. According to this view, death scenes described in literature or acted out on the stage were not enough to satisfy the gnawing desire to decipher the mysteries surrounding death, in a sense to dissect and examine death, and thereby to understand it. And in the minds of many Romans, nothing could substitute for being close to and studying the real thing.

The bloody gladiatorial contests that so captivated Roman audiences were not, therefore, as has so often and too easily been suggested, simply expressions of public depravity and sadism. Rather, during these shows both the performers and spectators took part in ceremonies and rituals that were a part of deeply rooted social, religious, and ethical traditions and beliefs. Indeed, the crowds at the amphitheaters were attracted and thrilled as much by the honorable and heroic display of courage in the face of death as by the excitement of the danger and spectacle of the slaughter. And what was on one level a form of entertainment was beneath the surface a ritualistic public expression of some of the most powerful core beliefs and values of both the individual and society.

Becoming a Gladiator

The grim reality that gladiators had such low social status, as well as the unenviable duty to lay down their lives for their "betters," naturally raises the questions of why and how people became gladiators in the first place. The majority of arena warriors started out unfree, mostly as slaves, criminals, or war captives, all of whom were forced into the profession (although the more successful ones could and often did eventually earn or buy their freedom). An unknown number—certainly a minority—of gladiatorial recruits were free individuals who volunteered.

Some of these volunteers became involved because they had financial difficulties, for there was a sign-up bonus for such men and usually prize money for those (both free and unfree) who won in the arena. Other volunteers were perhaps motivated by the physical challenge and appeal of danger or the prospect of becoming popular idols and sex symbols who could have their pick of pretty young girls. Among the graffiti slogans still scrawled on the walls at Pompeii are "Caladus, the Thracian, makes all the girls sigh" and "Crescens, the net fighter, holds the hearts of all the girls."[44]

Until the mid–first century B.C., the unfree gladiatorial recruits were mostly procured by a wholesaler or middleman (the *lanista*). He scoured the countryside, islands, and markets far and wide looking for slaves or prisoners he could buy cheap. And, doubtless, many such wholesalers were not above dealing with pirates who raided distant shores and kidnapped whole families or villages. A *lanista* could make a considerable profit from selling or renting out his fighters, because the prominent republican officials who staged public shows—Julius Caesar for example—were willing to spend large sums to bolster their own public images. The downside for the wholesaler of gladiators was that his social status was little or no better than that of the persons he bought and sold. Most Romans, including those who dealt with him, looked on him as a vile and disreputable pimp.[45]

After Caesar's time, as the amphitheater games became larger in scope, the demand for new gladiatorial recruits grew apace. And the Roman state, which rapidly came to monopolize the procurement, maintenance, and training of gladiators, met that demand. When the Romans won a battle against a foreign people, for instance, they singled out an unspecified number of the prisoners—usually the healthiest and strongest—to become arena fighters. The state also obtained recruits of slave status by buying them from *lanistae* (who still traded in gladiators but were now required to supply games organizers with a certain number of recruits at a low price) in slave markets or from private owners who made extra money by selling or hiring out their slaves for the arena.[46] A criminal penalty known as the *damnatio ad ludum* (meaning "condemned to the gladiator barracks") was another important source of new gladiators. Some of the free individuals convicted of serious crimes (such as arson, military mutiny, murder, or treason) received this penalty rather than sentences of death or hard labor in the mines.

Schools and Discipline

By the early first century A.D., the imperial *ludi* (gladiator schools or barracks) were the only authorized training facilities for arena fighters (a rule that helped the state maintain its control of the profession). There were three imperial *ludi* in Rome—the *Ludus Gallicus, Ludus Dacicus,* and *Ludus Magnus.* The latter, begun by Domitian in the late first century and completed under Hadrian in the second, was located near the Colosseum and connected to the great amphitheater by an underground tunnel. Imperial barracks also existed outside the capital, in Italy and in all of the provinces. Commonly, the best fighters from these outlying areas were eventually summoned to perform in Rome before the emperor, whose *munera* were the largest and most prestigious.

Life in a gladiator barracks was harsh to say the least. First, the facilities themselves were cold, spare, and grim. Roland Auguet, a noted scholar of Roman games, describes the one at Pompeii, which Vesuvius's ash preserved remarkably well:

Should All Gladiators Be Forced to Serve Out Their Sentences?

The distinguished Roman legislator and writer Pliny the Younger (ca. A.D. 61–113) traveled to the province of Bithynia-Pontus (in Asia Minor) in 111 as a special representative of the emperor Trajan. One of the many exchanges of letters between the two, excerpted here (from Betty Radice's translation of Pliny's letters), concerns some criminals who had been condemned to become gladiators but had not completed their sentences.

Pliny to Trajan

"In several cities, notably Nicomedia and Nicaea, there are people who were sentenced to service in the mines or the arena . . . but are now performing the duties of public [i.e., state-owned] slaves and receiving an annual salary for their work.. . . I have long been debating what to do. I felt it was too hard on the men to send them back to work out their sentences after a lapse of many years, when most of them are old by now, and by all accounts are quietly leading honest lives, but I did not think it quite right to retain criminals in public service. . . . I was therefore obliged to leave the whole question in suspense until I could consult you."

Trajan to Pliny

"Let us not forget that the chief reason for sending you to your province was the evident need for many reforms. Nothing in fact stands more in need of correction than the situation described in your letter. . . . Those among them who were sentenced within the last ten years and were released by no proper authority must therefore be sent back to work out their sentences. But if the men are elderly and have sentences dating back more than ten years, they can be employed in work of a penal nature, cleaning public baths and sewers, or repairing streets and highways, the usual employment for men of this type."

The *ludus* received them [the recruits] in rows of cells, some without skylights, which lined the square where they exercised. It was a prison, or at least the most forbidding of barracks. . . . The cells ranged on two levels, were four yards long and without means of intercommunication. An immense kitchen, the far wall of which had a kitchen-range [hearth for cooking] along its whole length, occupied the center of one of the sides of the rectangle [central square]; there was a prison, in the exact sense of the term, and an armory.[47]

The prison at the Pompeiian *ludus* featured a ceiling so low that the inmates could only sit or lie down; it also had sturdy and surely painful leg irons. This and other evidence illustrate the perceived need for strict and harsh discipline to maintain control over the hundreds (and in the largest schools perhaps thousands) of residents, most of whom did not want to be there. No weapons were allowed in a barracks (hence the gladiators trained with wooden swords), for fear that the gladiators would kill themselves or a trainer, or worse—escape.

The most notorious such breakout occurred in 73 B.C., when a group of slaves at a gladiator school in Capua, about a hundred miles south of Rome, escaped and began terrorizing the surrounding countryside. According to Plutarch, the men

> had done nothing wrong, but, simply because of the cruelty of their owner, were kept in close confinement until the time came for them to engage in combat. Two hundred of them planned to escape, but their plan was betrayed and only seventy-eight . . . managed to act in time and get away, armed with choppers and spits which they seized from some cookhouse.[48]

Under an unusually capable leader named Spartacus, these gladiators freed many slaves in central Italy, built a formidable army from their ranks, and defeated several small Roman armies sent against them.

Eventually, however, the Roman government appointed a wealthy aristocrat, Marcus Crassus, to quell the uprising. And in 71, he caught up with the rebels in the southern Italian region of Lucania. There, the slaves staged a heroic last stand but ultimately went down to defeat. Spartacus and most of his followers died in the battle, and the six thousand surviving slaves were crucified along the road to Rome as a warning to others who might contemplate threatening the established order. After Spartacus, Rome had no more major gladiatorial or slave rebellions, but the authorities remained ever fearful and vigilant.

Training and Health Care

The training that individuals like Spartacus underwent in the *ludi* was comprehensive and rigorous. The instructors (*doctores*) were highly specialized, each an expert in some kind of weaponry or style of fighting. The *doctor thracicum*, for example, knew the ins and outs of fighting with the curved Thracian short sword, the *sica*. Not surprisingly, the majority of these teachers were former gladiators who had grown too old to fight and either could not find or cared not to seek a life outside the profession.

The *doctores* drilled both recruits and veterans in the school's rectangular central yard. Keeping a close eye on their pupils, the instructors barked orders (*dictata*) at them, correcting mistakes made in footwork, lunges, parries, feints, and other subtleties of arena fighting. A trainee spent a good deal of time attacking a stationary six-foot-tall wooden pole, the *palus*, which represented an opponent, as well as dueling with other trainees. Eventually, the training pole lent its name to various groups or squads of gladiators in the school. The most skilled (and therefore the most respected and envied) belonged to the *primus palus*, the second best to the *secundus palus*, and so forth.

It must be noted that amid all the confinement, harsh discipline, and relentless and demanding physical drills, which might seem inhumane by modern standards, the *ludi*'s staffs paid close attention to the health of their residents. These schools, historian Michael Grant writes in his noted treatise on gladiators,

> were judiciously situated in favorable climates, and equipped with first-class doctors. Indeed, in the second century A.D. one of the most famous medical men of all time, Galen of Pergamum . . . served as a gladiators' doctor in his native Asia Minor . . . before rising to the position of [the emperor] Marcus Aurelius's personal physician. When he was working with these fighters, Galen claimed that his attention to their health and horrible wounds was re-

The Greatest Gladiator Rebellion

One of the most famous, and for a time the most feared, of Roman gladiators was Spartacus, who led the last of Rome's great slave rebellions in the 70s B.C. This account of the uprising's opening stages is from Plutarch's *Life of Crassus*, written about a century and a half later.

"The rising of the gladiators and their devastation of Italy, which is generally known as the war of Spartacus, began as follows. A man called Lentulus Batiatus had an establishment for gladiators at Capua. Most of them were Gauls [from central Europe] and Thracians [from northern Greece]. They had done nothing wrong, but, simply because of the cruelty of their owner, were kept in close confinement until the time came for them to engage in combat. Two hundred of them planned to escape, but their plan was betrayed and only seventy-eight . . . managed to act in time and get away, armed with choppers and spits which they seized from some cookhouse. On the road they came across some wagons which were carrying arms for gladiators to another city, and they took these arms for their own use. They then occupied a strong position and elected three leaders. The first [chief] of these was Spartacus. He was a Thracian from the nomadic tribes and not only had a great spirit and great physical strength, but was, much more than one would expect from his condition [i.e., slavery], most intelligent and cultured. . . . First, then, the gladiators repulsed those [troops] who came out against them from Capua. In this engagement they got hold of proper arms and gladly took them in exchange for their own gladiatorial equipment, which they threw away, as being barbarous and dishonorable weapons to use. Then the praetor Clodius, with some 3,000 soldiers, was sent out against them from Rome. He laid siege to them in a position which they took up on a hill. . . . The gladiators were able to get round behind them and to throw them into confusion by the unexpectedness of their attack, first routing them and then capturing their camp."

sponsible for a substantial reduction of mortality. The schools were also provided with resident medical consultants to check the men's diet. . . . Inscriptions also record the services of skilled masseurs *(unctores)*.[49]

At some point, each trainee must have hoped that his months (or in some cases years) of weapons training and physical regimen had prepared him well for the few moments he would spend in the arena. For if he slacked off in any area of preparation, he might well end up as a corpse lying in the blood-soaked sand. The grim reality was that in most gladiatorial combats, two fighters marched into the arena, but only one marched out.

CHAPTER 4 Gladiators: Their Mortal Combats

Like his life in the dismal barracks, a gladiator's appearance in the arena was a formal, regimented affair, scripted by custom, ceremony, and accepted rules of conduct. The gladiator entered the arena at a prescribed place and time; automatically took part in the often elaborate preliminary rituals; began fighting when the appropriate signal was given; and, if he survived, exited the arena where and when he was told. No deviations from these procedures or any sort of protests or appeals for leniency were possible. Such insolence would have led to almost immediate execution.

Moreover, while in the amphitheater, the gladiator was in a sense the plaything of the emperor (or other highest ranking leader present) and the spectators. And entertaining and appeasing them was as essential to the fighter's well-being as defeating his opponent, for if his performance was viewed as substandard, he could be flogged or even killed. He had, after all, taken an oath to fight and die for his "betters," and to break that oath would be to trample in the dust the only badge of honor to which he could lay claim. Thus, the gladiator, trapped by circumstance and tradition, had no choice but to observe the amphitheater's rules and customs closely and to fight as vigorously and skillfully as he could.

The Various Kinds of Gladiators

On the eagerly anticipated day when a *munus* was scheduled at the Colosseum or

This impressive Roman mosaic depicts various participants in the amphitheater shows, including gladiators, musicians, and the games official (behind podium).

A Samnite warrior, as depicted on a vase. The Samnite gladiator bore similar armor and weapons.

other amphitheater, the gladiators first entered the arena in a colorful parade known as the *pompa.* This was similar in some ways to the procession of the athletes on opening day of the modern Olympic Games, though usually on a considerably smaller scale. The fighters were usually accompanied by jugglers, acrobats, and other performers, and all kept time to marching music played on trumpets, flutes, drums, and sometimes a large hydraulic organ. (The musicians probably also played during the actual fighting, producing the same effect as the background musical score of a movie.)

During the *pompa,* the audience had its first chance to see not only how many fighters would be taking part in the day's games, but also what kinds, for there were various types and categories of gladiators. One of the four main types that had evolved by the early Empire was the heavily armed Samnite, later called a *hoplomachus* or *secutor.* (The Romans may have recognized these three terms as separate and distinct types, but any such distinctions are now unclear; all employed basically the same weapons and tactics.) He carried a sword or a lance and a *scutum* (the rectangular shield used by Roman legionary soldiers), and wore a metal helmet, and protective armor on his right arm and left leg.

Of the three other major gladiator types, the Thracian (so named because he resembled fighters from Thrace, a region of northern Greece) was less elaborately armed. He wielded a curved short sword, the *sica,* and a small round shield, the *parma.* The *myrmillo,* or "fishman" (after the fish-shaped crest on his helmet) was apparently similar to a Samnite, but less heavily armed. Usually (but certainly not always), a *myrmillo* fought the fourth most common kind of warrior, the *retiarius,* or "net-wielder," who wore no armor at all. A *retiarius* attempted to ensnare his opponent in his net (or used the net to trip the other man) and then stab him with a long, razor-sharp trident (a three-pronged spear). Accompanying the traditional rivalry between *myrmillones* and *retiarii* was the tale of the net-wielder who supposedly yelled at a retreating fishman, "It is not you I am trying to catch, it's your fish; why do you run away?"[50]

In addition to the pairings of these main gladiator types, there were a number of special and offbeat types and pairings. These included the *dimachaeri,* who fought without shields, instead wielding two swords (or daggers), one in each hand; the *laquearii,* whose

Gladiators in the Movies

Unfortunately, few film depictions of ancient Roman gladiatorial combats have been accurately costumed or staged. Two of the notable exceptions were *Demetrius and the Gladiators* (1954, directed by Delmer Davies) and *Spartacus* (1960, directed by Stanley Kubrick). In *Demetrius*, the title character (played by Victor Mature) is a former Greek slave condemned to train at a gladiator school in Rome. At first, because he is a Christian, he refuses to fight. But when one of his friends is apparently killed by a gladiator, he changes his mind. Dressed as a *myrmillo* or *secutor*, with helmet, short sword, and shield, he faces and defeats a *retiarius*, armed with net and trident, in an exhibition before the corrupt emperor Caligula (ruled A.D. 37–41); he then goes on to defeat three other opponents simultaneously in an exciting arena battle.

In *Spartacus*, the title character (played by Kirk Douglas) is the real-life gladiator who led a huge slave rebellion against the Roman state in the first century B.C. Before escaping the gladiator school to which he was brought in chains, he is forced to fight a fellow trainee in a small arena to gratify a group of Roman aristocrats who are visiting the school. Spartacus is arrayed as a Thracian, with an exposed chest, small round shield (*parma*), and curved sword (*sica*), while his opponent is a *retiarius*. Although the latter defeats Spartacus in the duel, he refuses to slay the fallen man and soon suffers death for his insolence. This scene, like the one in *Demetrius*, impressively re-creates the spectacle, excitement, and brutality of the Roman arena.

Actor Kirk Douglas portrays the famous Spartacus, who is dressed as a Thracian gladiator.

main offensive weapon was a lasso, with which one apparently tripped or entangled an opponent and then choked him (or perhaps finished him off with a dagger); the *equites*, who fought on horseback using lances, swords, and/or lassos; the *essedarii*, who confronted each other from moving chariots; and perhaps the most bizarre of the lot, the *andabates*, who grappled while blindfolded by massive helmets with no eye holes. There were still other types of gladiators, which are mentioned in inscriptions—for example, the *scissores* (carvers)—but nothing is known about them except for their names.

"Those About to Die Salute You!"

Following the *pompa,* the acrobats and other minor performers exited. Then the gladiators proceeded, in full public view, to draw lots, which decided who would fight whom. The drawing was supervised by the *munerarius* (or *editor*), the public magistrate charged with financing and staging the games. There may well have been a number of separate drawings. For instance, it is probable that experienced veterans usually drew only against one another, for as Auguet points out, "There would have been no point in opposing a veteran . . . and some novice who had not yet had even a single victory. Furthermore, the gladiator himself would have judged it dishonorable to be paired with an adversary not of his stature."[51]

After the pairings had been decided, the *munerarius* (or on occasion some distinguished guest or even the emperor himself) inspected the fighter's weapons to make sure they were sound and well sharpened. This process was called the *probatio armorum* ("approval," "proof," or "test" of arms). Like so many other customs of the arena, it probably derived from some early solemn ceremony of Etruscan funeral ritual. The last part of the preliminary arena ceremony consisted of a formal salute to the highest ranking official present—if not the emperor, usually the *munerarius*. The gladiators soberly raised their weapons toward the official and recited the phrase "*Morituri te salutant!*" ("Those about to die salute you!").

Finally, the first pairing began. No detailed, blow-by-blow description of a match has survived, but Auguet's believable reconstruction of a bout between a *retiarius* and a *secutor,* excerpted below, gives an idea of some of the typical strategies and moves, as well as the desperation and ferocity of the fighting.

> Apart from retreat, his [the *retiarius's*] sole means of defense was attack; as soon as he had gained enough ground to turn without danger, he was once more on the attack, his body twisted slightly to the left by the trident which he thrust out before him, head down, to keep his adversary at a distance. In his right hand he balanced a net, which he swung round in a circular

These bronze statuettes depict two gladiators, probably secutores, *fighting. The shields they originally held have not survived.*

movement. But as soon as he had thrown it, his adversary ducked, raising the shield which he held in his left hand to the level of his eyes. . . . As soon as the dry rattle of the [net's] meshes against the metal had warned him that he was safe, [the *secutor*] counterattacked, sword in hand; but now the *retiarius* had no time to recover his net before running away. It was a first step towards defeat for, well thrown, his weapon could by itself decide the issue of combat. . . . The loss of his net forced the *retiarius* to change his tactics; he seized the trident in both hands, the left hand near the prongs and right gripping the end of the shaft. Thus stationed, he at first kept the *secutor* at bay by the full length of his weapon, then attacked, thrusting the trident violently downward as if to pin a monster to the ground. . . . The *secutor* parried the blows with his sword rather than by using his shield. . . . He was trying to make it [the trident] fall from the hands of the *retiarius* and, with this in view, went so far as to use his shield as an offensive weapon; seizing the moment of an attack from below, he thrust it down on the inclined shaft, throwing his whole weight upon it, to make his adversary lose his grip. The latter, forced to draw aside to avoid the sword threatening his flank [side] . . . had great difficulty in breaking away. Parrying one of his adversary's blows on the left, he caught the *secutor*'s shield on the right and he succeeded in tearing it away; but, thrown off balance by the effort, the two men rolled on the ground and the trident flew several yards away. They did not think of recovering their arms but threw themselves on each other, crawling over the sand in a sort of duel with knives.[52]

Meanwhile, the spectators, like those at modern boxing matches and bullfights, reacted excitedly. Typical shouted phrases included "*Verbera!*" (Strike!), "*Habet!*" (A hit!), "*Hoc habet!*" (Now he's done for!), and "*Ure!*" (Burn him up!).

Win, Lose, or Draw

No matter what the pairing of gladiator types or specific strategies and moves involved, a bout had several possible outcomes. The most common of these were indicated in a careful list made at the conclusion of each *munus*.

This shot from an early version of Quo Vadis *shows a victorious gladiator awaiting the life-or-death decision of the games official.*

The listings consisted of the fighters' names, followed by the appropriate letters, including *P* (for *periit*, "perished"), *V* (for *vicit*, "won"), or *M* (for *missus*, denoting a loser who was allowed to live and fight another day). This indicates that a fighter could win by either killing his opponent outright or decisively incapacitating him in some way (by wounding him or stripping him of his weapons).

On the other hand, if both warriors fought bravely and could not best each other, the *munerarius* declared the bout a draw, and each gladiator was described as *stans missus*. That this was a fairly common outcome is shown by its frequent mention in inscriptions. The epitaph of a fighter named Flamma, for example, claims that in his thirty-eight bouts he won twenty-five times, was *missus* four times, and *stans missus* nine times. When each combatant was *stans missus*, prizes (palm branches and money, awarded in front of the crowd) could be given to neither or to both. In an epigram designed to court the favor of his patron, Domitian, Martial recorded a draw that ended with both fighters receiving a prize:

> As Priscus and Verus each drew out the contest and the struggle between the pair long stood equal, [the crowd's loud and frequent shouts] sought discharge for the combatants. But Caesar [a reference to Domitian, the name Caesar by now having become an imperial title] obeyed his own law (the law was that the bout go on without shield until a finger was raised [the signal from one fighter that he surrendered]). . . . But an end to the even strife was found: equal, they fought, equal, they yielded. To both, Caesar sent wooden swords [like those they had trained with, in this case symbolizing their discharge from service] and to both palms. Thus valor and skill had their reward. This has happened under no prince but you, Caesar: two fought and both won.[53]

In another, and mercifully less common, kind of combat, the *sine missione*, draws were not allowed. The gladiators had to keep fighting, no matter how long it took, until one was killed. (Augustus banned this practice, thinking it cruel, but other emperors later revived it.)

Sometimes both officials and spectators felt that the fighters were not giving it their all. In his famous novel *The Satyricon*, the first-century A.D. writer Petronius (Gaius Petronius Arbiter) has a character complain:

> What good has Norbanus [a politician who staged a gladiator show] done us? He put on some half-pint gladiators, so done-in already that they'd have dropped if you blew on them. I've seen animal killers [most of whom had little or no training] fight better. . . . One boy did have a little spirit—he was in Thracian armor [i.e., carried a Thracian sword and shield], and even he didn't show any initiative. In fact, they were all flogged afterwards [for failing to fight well], there were so many shouts of "Give 'em what for!" from the crowd. Pure yellow [cowardice], that's all.[54]

Or even worse, on occasion one fighter actually turned and ran for his life. "Officiosus fled on November 6 in the consulate of Drusus Caesar and M. Junius Norbanus,"[55] reads a Pompeiian inscription. Such offenders were punished by whipping, branding with hot irons, or immediate execution.

When one gladiator went down wounded, as happened frequently in these mortal combats, he was allowed to raise one finger, a sign of appeal for mercy. At that fateful moment, he was not allowed to move or to touch his

In this combat, one contestant has dropped his shield and appeals for mercy from the games' official.

weapons. If he did grab a weapon and attempt to resume the fight, which happened on extremely rare occasions, he customarily incurred the wrath of the highest ranking official present and also the crowd, which almost always booed and cursed him. (Suetonius recorded an incident in which a group of *retiarii* fought a group of *secutores* before the emperor Caligula. After the net-wielders had lost, one of them seized a trident and slew the victors one by one, prompting the emperor to condemn his action as "murder.")[56]

Most of the time the emperor or *munerarius* decided a downed fighter's fate, usually in accordance with the crowd's wishes. The traditional consensus among modern historians has been that if the spectators desired a fighter spared, they signaled their desire with a "thumbs-up" gesture, whereas if their choice was death, they indicated it with a "thumbs-down." This may indeed be the case. However, several experts have offered other intriguing possibilities, such as a "thumbs-down" (along with the waving of handkerchiefs) as the signal for the victor to drop his sword and spare the loser, and the pressing of the thumb toward the chest (symbolizing a sword through the heart) to call for death. Although the exact nature of the gestures themselves remains unresolved, it is more certain that the crowd also shouted phrases such as "*Mitte!*" (Spare him!) or "*Iugula!*" (Cut his throat!) to emphasize their wishes.

Still another possible outcome of a combat was when a fallen combatant pretended to be dead. Few, if any, were successful at this ruse, however, because men dressed like the Etruscan demon Charun (another retained

The emperor and empress give the dreaded "thumbs-down" in this fanciful modern drawing.

custom illustrating the games' Etruscan roots) ran out and applied hot irons to the bodies. Any fakers exposed in this way promptly had their throats cut. When a match ended in death, in this or any other way, men dressed as the god Mercury (transporter of the dead) ran out and whisked away the corpses, then a team of boys cleaned the blood stains from the sand to prepare the arena for the next round of battles.

Those Condemned to Outright Execution

The gladiatorial bouts were not the only amphitheater spectacles in which people died. Interspersed with the *munera* and other arena events (including the wild beast shows) were "attractions" featuring the massacre of completely or almost completely helpless humans. Although these were by no means a part of the *munera* in the strict sense, gladiators were often involved in them. It is important to understand the distinction between formal gladiatorial fights, which involved trained fighters, and what were essentially public executions of ordinary people.

While various criminals might be sentenced to the gladiator schools, many serious offenders were sentenced instead to outright death in the arena (making them *noxii ad gladium ludi damnati,* "condemned to be killed by the sword in the games"). The *munerarius* took charge of these condemned persons, guaranteeing that each would be killed within a year. Usually at around noon, before the formal gladiatorial bouts had begun, guards herded the unarmed criminals up onto the arena floor, where some were quickly hacked down by a troop of fully armed gladiators. Others were crucified. And still others were tied to stakes on which they were mangled and eaten by half-starved lions, bears, and other beasts. Often during these massacres, attendants veiled any emperors' statues adorning the amphitheater, symbolically sparing them the sight of "riff-raff" in their death throes. Supposedly, the emperor Claudius (reigned A.D. 41–54) ordered so many such executions that he had a statue of Augustus removed so that it would not have to be constantly veiled.

Perhaps the most famous Roman lawbreaker summarily executed before an amphitheater audience was the notorious brigand and murderer Laureolus. His gruesome punishment was the subject of a mime, or short dramatic presentation, composed by the poet Gaius Valerius Catullus in the first century B.C. Beginning about A.D. 30, actors periodically staged re-creations of Laureolus's execution before crowds in various amphitheaters. And in the Colosseum, beginning in Domitian's reign, at the play's climax a condemned criminal took the actor's place and suffered a real execution that was guaranteed to satisfy the most jaded of spectators. The unfortunate individual was nailed to a cross and then, while still alive and conscious, mutilated and eaten by a bear. Martial captured this grisly event:

> Laureolus, hanging on no sham cross, gave his naked flesh to a Caledonian bear. His lacerated limbs lived on, dripping gore, and in all his body, body there was none [i.e., his body had lost its normal shape]. Finally he met with the punishment he deserved; the guilty wretch had plunged a sword into his father's throat or his master's, or in his madness had robbed a temple of its secret gold, or laid a cruel torch to Rome. The criminal had outdone the misdeeds of ancient story; in him, what had been a play became an execution.[57]

Did Christians Die in the Arena?

Although firm documented evidence is lacking, it is likely that some early Christians were among those who were condemned to public execution in the Roman Colosseum. According to tradition, the first Christian who died in the great amphitheater was Saint Ignatius, bishop of Antioch, the first writer to refer to the church as "catholic," or universal. Supposedly, he welcomed martyrdom in the arena and exclaimed shortly before his death, "I am as the grain of the field, and must be ground by the teeth of the lions, that I may become fit for His [God's] table."

It should be noted, however, that the popular notion that the Romans were religiously intolerant and persecuted the Christians for having different beliefs is mistaken. By the mid–first century A.D., when Christianity was first spreading through the Empire, the highly tolerant Romans had welcomed and themselves practiced numerous alternative and often exotic religions from around the Mediterranean world. All of these flourished alongside Rome's state religion, which venerated traditional gods like Jupiter, Juno, and Minerva.

What made the early Christians different was their own intolerance. In addition to condemning all other beliefs but their own, many of them refused to acknowledge the emperor's authority, which disturbed the traditionally highly patriotic Romans. Moreover, the Christians kept to themselves, appearing to be antisocial, and over time they acquired the terrible stigma of having *odium generis humani*, a "hatred for the human race." Worst of all, unfounded rumors spread claiming that Christian rituals included cannibalism, incest, and other repugnant acts. Most Romans came to believe these fables and therefore felt little or no pity for any of the Christians who may have met their deaths on the arena's blood-soaked sands.

Substitutes for Laureolus continued to die in this same manner in the Colosseum and other amphitheaters across the Empire until at least A.D. 200.

Some Moral and Intellectual Objections

If the manner of these executions seems extreme in modern eyes, it must be remembered that the average Roman not only took capital punishment for granted but also saw public humiliation as a fitting penalty for many crimes (and maybe also as a deterrent to crime in general). Therefore, many of those who attended the amphitheater games found it perfectly acceptable for murderers and other serious criminals to suffer public execution in the arena.

By contrast, some Romans did view such killings (and maybe gladiatorial fights and other kinds of arena bloodletting as well) as distasteful. Exactly how many and what types of people felt this way remains unclear. Perhaps it was more often than not the better-educated members of society, although admittedly this is no more than an assumption based on the fact that most of the surviving evidence consists of the testimony of upper-class intellectuals like Cicero and Seneca. That Seneca disliked at least some aspects of the killing that went on in amphitheaters is clear from his disdainful description of the slaughter of a group of unarmed condemned men:

> I happened on the noon interlude at the arena, expecting some clever burlesque, some relaxation to give the spectators a respite [break] from human gore. [But] the show was the reverse. The fighting that had gone before [i.e., the regular gladiatorial fights] was charity by contrast. Now there was no nonsense about it; it was pure murder. The men have nothing to protect them; the whole body is exposed and every stroke tells. Many spectators prefer this to the usual matches. Why shouldn't they? There is no helmet or shield to parry the steel. Why armor? Why skill? Such things [merely] delay the [inevitable] kill.[58]

Sharing these feelings was the second-century A.D. emperor Marcus Aurelius, who thoroughly disliked the butchery of both humans and beasts. Attending the Colosseum strictly out of a sense of duty to his subjects, he often ignored the games and utilized the time by dictating letters and conducting other state business.

Other intellectual types either thought the butchery of the arena beneath their "refined" tastes or found them just plain boring. Cicero and some of his friends evidently fell into this group. Congratulating one such friend, Marcus Marius, for not attending a large-scale spectacle in 55 B.C., Cicero (who attended out of feelings of obligation to the man who staged it) wrote:

> If it was some physical ailment or ill health which kept you from attending the spectacles, I would attribute your absence more to your luck than to your wisdom. But if you decided to scorn what other men marvel at, and chose not to attend, although good health would have allowed you to, then I have two reasons to be delighted: first, because you were free from physical pain and, second, because your mind was strong, since you ignored things other men marvel at for no reason. . . . All and all, the entertainments were (if you're interested) quite splendid, but certainly not to your taste. . . . The spectacle of such extravagant expense destroyed any spontaneous merriment. . . . Things which won the applause of the common people would have given you no enjoyment. . . . I know that you certainly didn't worry about missing the athletes, since you have always been scornful of gladiators.[59]

It must be granted, however, that the supremely educated Seneca, Aurelius, and Cicero were far from being typical Romans. And there is little doubt that most of their countrymen, for centuries to come, had few or no objections—moral, intellectual, or otherwise—to gladiators killing either one another or condemned criminals. Only much later (in the mid–fourth century), when the Christians came to wield considerable political power in Rome, did such objections begin to become widespread. Eventually, they would manage to eradicate altogether the time-honored *munera* and the gladiator schools that supplied them.

CHAPTER 5

Wild Animal Shows and Staged Naval Battles

Though immensely popular, gladiators were by no means the only popular attractions of Roman amphitheaters. There were also a wide variety of animal shows, collectively known as *venationes* (singular, *venatio*), or "hunts." (The term *hunt* is a bit of a misnomer, since none of these consisted of sportsmen stalking wild creatures in their natural habitats; *fights* would be a more accurate way of describing most of them.) Though technically classified as *ludi,* the hunts came to be associated with the *munera*, mainly because they were usually presented on the same program with gladiatorial bouts in the amphitheater or elsewhere.

Originally (throughout the second and well into the first century B.C.), the *venationes* were minor spectacles presented generally in the morning. Because this was when most Romans were busy working or attending to personal affairs, the morning audiences tended to be small. But the hunts became increasingly popular, and by the late Republic and early Empire the larger-scale *venationes* were staged in the afternoon, drew big crowds, and sometimes lasted for several days.

Though the hunts that featured hundreds of animals and humans, sometimes in elaborate artificially constructed settings, were undeniably spectacular, they were dwarfed by the largest of all Roman public shows—the *naumachiae*. These were full-scale sea battles staged most often on lakes, both real and artificial. Because they were expensive to create, the *naumachiae* appeared much less regularly than either the *munera* or *venationes*. Also, the sea fights remained in vogue for only a relatively brief period. Whereas games featuring gladiators and animals were presented almost continuously for five or six centuries, the *naumachiae* enjoyed a heyday of only about a century and a half (first appearing under Caesar in the late Republic and becoming an extremely rare event after about A.D. 100).

Remarkable Performing Animals

No other kind of Roman spectacle had as many forms and variations as the animal shows, which were staged not only in amphitheaters but in circuses, town squares, and wherever else suitable space could be found. In their totality, these shows involved almost every animal familiar to the ancient Romans in a wide array of public exhibitions. For the sake of convenience, however, they can be grouped into four general categories: those in which exotic animals were exhibited or in which trained animals performed; those in which trained "hunters" fought and killed animals; those in which animals fought and killed one another; and those in which prisoners were executed by exposure to half-starved beasts. (It should be noted that one large-scale *venatio* might feature a mix of several or all of these categories.)

Bloodless exhibitions of exotic animals were popular in Rome even before the *venationes* existed. Perhaps because they began as

An arena "hunter" is attacked by a lion in this engraving based on a sculpture.

a pastoral people, the Romans had long been fascinated by and fond of animals. And eventually, as Rome's power extended over new and more distant foreign territories, it became customary for generals to bring back sample creatures from other lands and display them in their triumphs (victory parades). Thus, Rome's inhabitants first saw elephants (which they nicknamed "Lucanian cows") in 275 B.C. when a few of the great beasts marched in the triumph of M. Curius Denatus, who had recently captured them after fighting the famed Greek general Pyrrhus. (Invited by a city then at odds with Rome, Pyrrhus had landed in Italy with a large army that included several war elephants.) Not long after 200 B.C., ostriches (nicknamed "sea sparrows"), leopards ("African mice"), and lions made their first appearance in Italy; the first hippopotamus and crocodile appeared in 58 B.C.; the first rhinoceros in 55 B.C.; and the first giraffe (perhaps a gift from Cleopatra to Julius Caesar) in 46 B.C. By Nero's time (mid–first century A.D.) the Romans regularly imported dozens of other exotic species, occasionally including polar bears and seals.

Some of these animals became pets. By the early Empire, for example, monkeys were fairly common Roman house pets; some well-to-do individuals kept leopards, lions, and even elephants as pets. Most such creatures, however, were exhibited or exploited in the public shows. Rome had no formal zoo in the modern sense, so animal exhibitions took place on an individual and irregular basis in venues ranging from public squares to amphitheaters. Among the more popular trained animals were monkeys, who were often dressed as soldiers and drove miniature chariots drawn by goats; dogs (Plutarch personally witnessed one that believably feigned eating poison, dying, and then returning to life); lions, which held rabbits, cats, and even mice in their jaws without harming them; bears, which climbed poles and performed other feats; and seals, which were frequently trained to answer to their names.

The favorite of all the trained animals was the elephant, and a number of surviving Roman stories describe its intelligence, nobility, and diligence in training. In one public show, a group of six male and six female pachyderms entered the arena, where tables had been set for dinner; amazingly well trained, they proceeded to recline and eat and drink like humans, displaying polite manners throughout the performance. Other elephants danced and walked tightropes. Perhaps the most remarkable and moving of all Roman elephants was the creature described by the noted scholar and writer Pliny the Elder (Gaius Plinius Secundus, A.D. 23–79). "It is a known fact," he writes, "that one elephant, somewhat slow-witted in understanding orders, was often beaten with a lash and was discovered at night practicing what he had to do."[60]

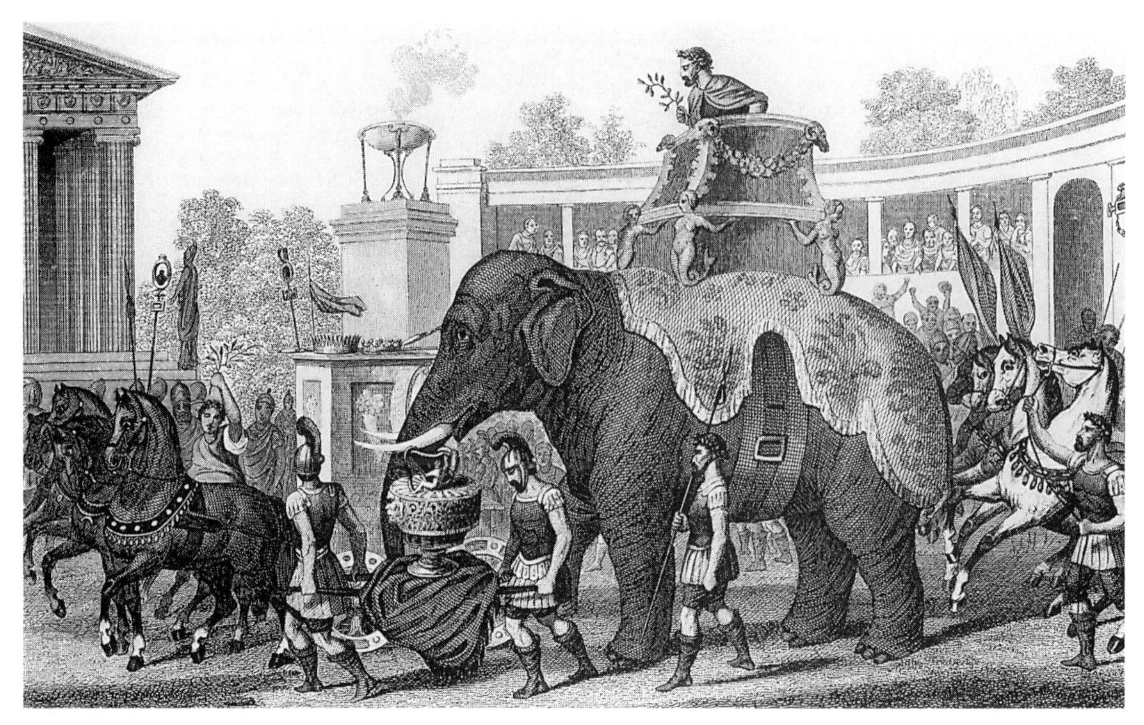

The Romans first encountered elephants in battle. Here, the famous Carthaginian general Hannibal rides a war elephant in a victory parade after a battle against the Romans.

Capturing and Transporting the Animals

Sadly, the majority of the animals gathered for Roman public shows did not end up as pets or charming performers. Huge numbers were maimed and killed in the *venationes*, so thousands of replacements of various species were needed on a regular basis. The animal acquisition process was complex, time-consuming, and involved hundreds and at times thousands of people of various backgrounds and skills. It was therefore extremely expensive, which explains why only the richest individuals or the government could afford to stage large-scale animal hunts (and indeed, by the early Empire, the *venationes* were virtually an imperial monopoly like the *munera*).

First, highly skilled hunters captured the animals in all parts of the known world. Elephants came from distant India or (more commonly) northern and central Africa; lions and leopards from Africa and Syria; bears from Africa, central Europe, and Italy itself; tigers from India and northern Persia; horses from Spain; exotic hounds (including Irish wolfhounds) from Britain; and crocodiles from Egypt. In most cases, the beasts were ensnared by leg traps, caught in pits, or driven into cages or nets. Describing how elephants were captured, Pliny the Elder wrote,

> In India, they are rounded up by a mahout [elephant driver], who, riding a tame elephant, either catches a wild one on its own, or separates one from the herd and beats it so that when it is exhausted he can

> mount it and control it in the same way as the tame one. Africans employ covered pits to trap elephants. When one strays into a pit, the rest of the herd immediately heap branches together, roll down rocks, and . . . [use] every effort to drag it out.[61]

The hunters delivered the captured animals to middlemen, who in turn handed them over to transporters for the journey to Rome (or other cities giving beast shows). Once at the destination city, the animals were kept in a holding area (*vivarium*) for an unspecified time and cared for until they reached the end of their journey (and often the end of their lives) in the amphitheater.

The total journey, from capture to arena, often took weeks or even months. All the while the animals had to be well fed and also closely watched to make sure they did not get loose. In one unfortunate incident, a leopard escaped its cage on a dock near Rome and killed a sculptor who was attempting to make a clay model of a caged lion. More notorious was the case of a shipment of lions that passed through the Greek city of Megara on its way to Rome in 48 B.C. The city came under attack by some of Caesar's troops, and as Plutarch tells it, the lions

> are said to have brought disaster to Megara, because when the city was on the point of being captured, the Megarians broke open the cages and unchained them, hoping that they would attack the enemy as they entered the city. But, instead of this, the lions turned against the unarmed Megarians and tore them to pieces as they ran to and fro in terror, so that even their enemies were overcome with pity at the sight.[62]

Capturing so many animals over the course of decades and centuries naturally tended to deplete their populations in certain areas; therefore, it became increasingly difficult to find some species. A hint of this problem, as well as the size and complexity of the animal acquisition process itself, is partially revealed in part of the surviving correspondence

A hunting party's efforts to capture wild animals in a net are the subject of this sculpture on a Roman sarcophagus (stone coffin).

The underground chambers of the Colosseum, once covered by the arena floor, are visible beneath the wooden safety railings in the lower right corner of this photo. These chambers housed the animals just prior to a venatio.

of Cicero when he served as governor of the province of Cilicia (in southern Asia Minor) from 51 to 50 B.C. In the summer of 51, his friend Marcus Caelius Rufus was elected aedile in Rome (giving him the responsibility of staging public entertainments, including animal shows). Once in office, Caelius immediately began begging Cicero to send him some Cilician panthers for his upcoming games. This is one exchange between the two men:

> [Caelius to Cicero]
>
> In almost all my letters to you I have written about the panthers. You will be embarrassed! Patiscus [a Roman businessman in Cilicia who enjoyed hunting] has sent Curio [a young public official in Rome] ten panthers, whereas you have not sent me the equivalent or more. And Curio gave those ten to me, plus another ten from Africa. . . . If you but remember, and if you send for some hunters . . . then you will satisfy my request. I am greatly concerned about this now, because I think I will have to make all the arrangements myself, without the help of my colleague. So please, dear friend, take on this task. . . . As soon as the panthers have been caught, you have with you the men I sent over on financial business to feed them and arrange for shipping.
>
> [Cicero to Caelius]
>
> About the panthers! The matter is being handled with diligence and according to my orders by men who are skillful hunters. But there is a remarkable scarcity of panthers. And they tell me that the few panthers left are complaining bitterly that they are the only animals in my province for whom traps are set. And therefore they have decided, or so the ru-

mor goes, to leave my province and move to Caria [a nearby region of Asia Minor]. But the matter is receiving careful attention. . . . Any animal found will be yours. But whether any will be found, we don't really know.[63]

The Hunters and Their Prey

One common fate of these creatures, once they had reached the arena, was to be pitted in mortal combat against a "hunter," or *venator*. (Another term for a hunter was *bestiarius,* meaning "beast-man." The two labels may have been more or less interchangeable, although many scholars believe that the term *bestiarii* referred either to lower-status hunters or people condemned to be killed by beasts or to hunters who used a different fighting style than that of the *venatores*.) Like gladiators, most *venatores* began as slaves and criminals, but a few were probably freeborn volunteers. They trained in a specialized school—the *ludus bestiariorum*—which no doubt resembled a typical gladiator barracks (although some evidence suggests that their training was less comprehensive and rigorous than that of gladiators).

This drawing is based on a famous statue of an arena fighter grappling with a lion.

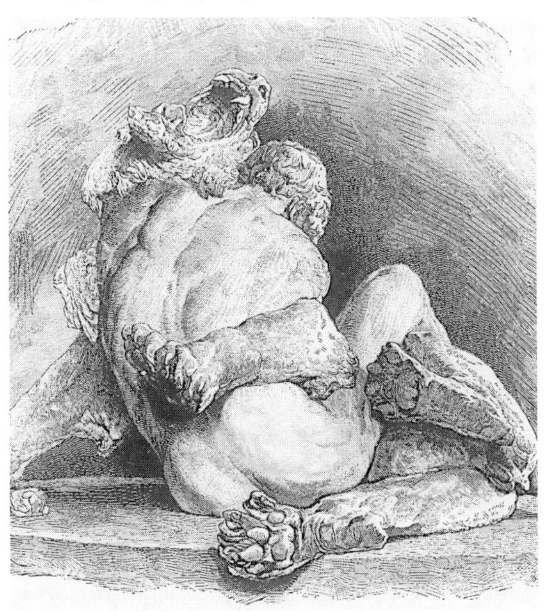

Perhaps the most common weapon the hunters wielded was a *venabulum*, a spear with an iron-reinforced point. However, all manner of other weapons were used as well, including swords, daggers, clubs, and bows and arrows. The fighters who specialized in killing with the bow were called *sagittarii.* Moreover, some hunters specialized in killing just one kind of animal, such as the *taurarii*, who, much like modern matadors, confronted bulls and attempted to stab them with lances. An exciting variation resembled a modern rodeo event; a hunter jumped from horseback onto the bull, grabbed its horns, and tried to wrestle it to the ground before killing it.

While these men slaughtered their prey, either singly or in groups, the crowds in the stands cheered them on. Not surprisingly, the most successful, colorful, and entertaining hunters became almost as popular with the public as the winning gladiators. One of the most widely acclaimed of all the *venatores* was a man named Carpophorus, who gained fame in the arena during Domitian's reign and on whom Martial heaped glowing praise in more than one epigram:

> He plunged his spear also in a charging bear, once prime in the peak of the Arctic pole [possibly a reference to a polar bear]; he laid low a lion of unprecedented size, a sight to see, who might have done honor to Hercules' hands [the mythical character Hercules was credited with slaying the powerful Nemean lion]; he stretched dead a fleet leopard with a wound felt from afar.[64]

Several venatores *struggle with a bull in a Roman arena. Tigers, leopards, giraffes, and hippopotamuses were also slaughtered in these shows.*

Over the course of time, the gruesome toll of animals butchered by Carpophorus and his fellow hunters must have been enormous. And of course to this toll must be added that of beasts killed in fights against other beasts. For example, "A tigress wont to lick the hand of the fearless trainer," Martial tells us, "fiercely tore a wild lion with rabid tooth; a novelty, unknown in any times. She dared do no such thing while she lived in the high forests, but since she has been among us she has gained ferocity."[65]

Some sample numbers give an idea of the scope of the carnage. Some 9,000 beasts died during the 100 days of Titus's inauguration of the Colosseum in A.D. 80; at least 11,000 were butchered in 107 when Trajan presented immense spectacles lasting 123 days; and in the games given in 248 by the emperor Philip the "Arab" (reigned 244–249) to celebrate the thousandth anniversary of Rome's founding, a partial list of the animals slaughtered supposedly included 32 elephants, 10 elk, 10 tigers, 70 lions, 30 leopards, 10 hyenas, 6 hippopotamuses, 1 rhin- oceros, 10 giraffes, 20 wild asses, and 40 wild horses. In all, during the nearly five or six centuries in which such shows remained popular, millions of animals must have met their doom.

A Certain Sympathy

When contemplating these large-scale slaughters, it is natural to ask why so many Romans viewed them as entertaining. As in the case of the *munera*, the phenomenon might be partially explained by a widespread fascination with death and its supposed mystical relation to life. A number of Martial's epigrams, for instance, seem to reflect, with a sort of awe, the belief that the lives and deaths of people and animals alike are often playthings in divine hands. Notable is a passage describing the emergence of an infant pig from its mother's womb at the moment of her death in the arena:

> A mother sow, struck by a heavy weapon and laid open by the wound, lost life and gave it at one and the same time. How sure was the hand that poised the steel! I

believe this hand was Lucina's [Lucina, a manifestation of Diana, goddess of the hunt, was thought by many to assist in childbirth]. Dying, the creature sampled the divine power of either Diana. By one the parent was delivered, by the other the beast was slain.[66]

Not every Roman saw the killing of animals (or of people by animals) as either fascinating or ethical. Although Cicero apparently had few qualms about human criminals fighting one another in the arena, he found the slaughter of helpless animals pitiful and disturbing. In a letter to his friend Marcus Marius, he recorded his feelings after attending a spectacle given by the famous military general Gnaeus Pompey (in 55 B.C.), in which six hundred lions and a number of elephants met their deaths:

There were wild animal hunts, two a day for five-days, very expensive ones—no one can deny that. But what pleasure can a civilized man find when either a helpless human being is mangled by a very strong animal, or a magnificent animal is stabbed again and again with a hunting spear? Even if this was something to look at, you have seen it often enough before, and I, who was a spectator there, saw nothing new. The last day was the day for elephants. The mob of spectators was greatly impressed, but showed no real enjoyment. In fact, a certain sympathy arose for the elephants, and a feeling that there was a kind of affinity between that large animal and the human race.[67]

Fighters Who Killed Themselves Rather than Others

In these excerpts from a letter to a friend (quoted in Hadas's *The Stoic Philosophy of Seneca*), Seneca describes two men—one from a beast show, the other from a *naumachia*—who took their own lives rather than participate in the games. Like other Stoics, Seneca believed that suicide was not only acceptable but an honorable means of escaping bondage.

"Do not imagine that only great men have had the toughness to break through the trammels of human bondage. . . . Men of the meanest condition have made a mighty effort to break through to deliverance . . . and by their own strength transformed implements naturally harmless into weapons. Lately a German in the beast- fighting barracks who was practicing for the morning show excused himself to relieve his bowels—the only function for which the guards would allow him privacy. Then he took the sponge-tipped stick used [to clean the latrines] and rammed it down his throat and choked his breath till he suffocated. That was a way to insult death! . . . Stout fellow, the right man to let choose his own fate! . . . On this all will agree: the dirtiest death is preferable to the daintiest slavery. . . . I promised you more examples from the same exhibitions. In the second event of a sea-fight spectacle one of the barbarians sank the whole spear which he was to use against his opponents down his own throat. 'Why', he cried, 'have I not long ago escaped all this torment, all this mockery?'. . . The show was the better worth looking at in the degree that men [and women who witness the act] learned that it is more decent to die than to kill."

Pliny the Elder provides more detail, some of it heartrending, about the treatment of the elephants in this same show. His description of the crowd's reactions corroborates that Cicero was far from alone in his conviction that these beasts suffered unnecessary cruelty:

> One elephant put up a fantastic fight and, although its feet were badly wounded, crawled on its knees against the attacking bands [of hunters]. It snatched away their shields and hurled them into the air. . . . There was also an extraordinary incident with a second elephant when it was killed by a single blow: a javelin struck under its eye and penetrated the vital parts of its head. All the elephants *en masse* [in a group], tried to break out through the iron railings that enclosed them, much to the discomfiture of the spectators. . . . But when Pompey's elephants had given up hope of escape, they played on the sympathy of the crowd, entreating [pleading with] them with indescribable gestures. They moaned, as if wailing, and caused the spectators such distress that, forgetting Pompey and his lavish display . . . they rose in a body, in tears, and heaped dire curses on Pompey, the effects of which he soon suffered.[68]

How Safe Were the Spectators?

The fact that the elephants in Pompey's show momentarily posed a real danger to the crowd draws attention to the issue of safety and security in the *venationes*. During republican times, the authorities apparently took only minimal precautions against wild animals escaping and injuring spectators. Pompey's "iron railings," for instance, were barely adequate. Beginning with Julius Caesar's games, however, better security measures were enacted, the major ones summarized here by the distinguished former Oxford University scholar J. P. V. D. Balsdon:

> When Caesar gave his great hunting games in the Circus Maximus in 46 B.C., a canal ten feet wide and ten feet deep was constructed, separating the audience from the arena. . . . The measures taken in Nero's amphitheater . . . were copied later in the Colosseum. The platform (*podium*) which surrounded the arena of the Colosseum, and above which the spectators' seats rose, was thirteen feet above ground level. At ground level between it and the arena itself was a wooden barricade from which at regular levels rose the tall masts for the awning. On these masts at a certain height were fixed elephant tusks, from which strong [protective] netting hung. As an additional precaution . . . there was an ivory cylinder, which rotated easily on its axis, at the foot of the *podium*, so that an animal which broke through would be frustrated if it tried to climb over it to reach the *podium*.[69]

In fact, no surviving records mention a spectator being injured or killed by an animal during a *venatio*; therefore, such occurrences were likely exceedingly rare.

Re-Creations of Sea Battles

It is not difficult to understand why Roman audiences were thrilled to attend the *naumachiae*. These full-scale re-creations of sea battles must have been truly spectacular, offering large numbers of ordinary people a glimpse of rare, larger-than-life events that even most sailors had never witnessed. (With

A large trireme—a warship with three banks of oars. The ships that fought in the naumachiae *were usually smaller, single-masted versions.*

the exception of the Battle of Actium in 31 B.C. and a few smaller and very occasional naval encounters, the Romans took part in no major sea battles after the Punic Wars of the third century B.C.)

These spectacles usually took place on lakes or in special basins (also called *naumachiae*) dug specifically to accommodate them. They also seem to have been held in amphitheaters whose arenas had been temporarily flooded. Martial called attention to the novelty of a sea battle staged by Domitian in the Colosseum:

> If you are from a distant land, a late spectator for whom this was the first day of the sacred show [i.e., a show given and attended by the emperor], let not the naval warfare deceive you with its ships, and the water like to [resembling] a sea: here but lately was land. You don't believe it? Watch while the waters weary Mars [i.e., the naval battle progresses]. But a short while hence you will be saying: "Here but lately was sea."[70]

This method appears to have been exceptional, however, partly because of the mechanical difficulties involved in filling and draining the arena, and was probably seen only on rare occasions in the larger amphitheaters. (Some scholars maintain that no amphitheaters were ever flooded in this manner. But if that is the case, how do we explain the apparently earnest descriptions of such events by Martial and several other ancient writers?) Even then, these facilities were not big enough to accommodate more than a handful of ships, hence the more frequent recourse to more expansive basins and lakes to stage full-scale battles.

The warships in these spectacles were manned by criminals and war captives, who, in the roles of sailors and soldiers in rival fleets, customarily fought to the death. Often, the fighters were outfitted to represent the participants of famous historical naval battles; the Greek-Persian encounter at Salamis (in 480 B.C.) was especially popular and often repeated. Caesar staged a *naumachia* in 46 B.C. in a basin dug in the Campus Martius. Some one thousand sailors and two thousand oarsmen, dressed as rival Egyptians and Phoenicians, took part. And Augustus held one of the most impressive such shows on record in 2 B.C., later bragging,

> I presented to the people an exhibition of a naval battle across the Tiber where a grove of the Caesars now is, having had the site excavated 1,800 feet in length and 1,200 feet in width. In this exhibition thirty beaked ships [i.e., equipped with rams], triremes [ships with three banks of oars] or biremes [with two banks], and in addition a great number of smaller vessels engaged in combat. On board these fleets, exclusive of rowers, there were about 3,000 combatants.[71]

The largest known *naumachia* of all was given by Claudius in A.D. 52. According to Tacitus,

> A tunnel through the mountain between the Fucine Lake and the River Liris [several miles southeast of Rome] had now been completed. To enable a large crowd to see this impressive achievement, a naval battle was staged on the lake itself, like the exhibition given by Augustus on his artificial lake adjoining the Tiber, though his ships and combatants had been fewer. Claudius equipped warships manned with nineteen thousand combatants, surrounding them with a circle of rafts to prevent their escape. Enough space in the middle, however, was left for energetic rowing, skillful steering, charging, and all the incidents of a seabattle. On the rafts were stationed double companies of the [Praetorian] Guard [the elite soldiers who guarded the emperor] and other units, behind ramparts [battlements] from which they could shoot catapults and stone-throwers. The rest of the lake was covered with the decked ships of the marines. The coast, the slopes, and the hill-tops were thronged like a theater by innumerable spectators, who had come from the neighboring towns and even from Rome itself—to see the show or pay respects to the emperor. Claudius presided in a splendid military cloak. . . . Though the fighters were criminals, they fought like brave men. After much bloodletting, they were spared extermination.[72]

The last *naumachia* mentioned in surviving ancient records is that presented by Philip the Arab at his millennial games in 248. Presumably the huge expense of these spectacles made any further attempts to stage them impractical. Then, too, they probably just went out of style, for in retrospect they seem an artifact of the exuberant days of the early Empire, when Roman resources and energies appeared (deceptively it turned out) inexhaustible. Indeed, they were largely an extravagant novelty, little missed once they were gone. After all, audiences still had plenty of gladiators and wild beasts to amuse them, as well as their all time favorite spectacle—chariot racing.

CHAPTER 6

The Circus Charioteers and Their Fans

The *ludi circenses*, Rome's most popular and long-lasting public spectacles, were so expensive to stage that they were held in Rome only a few days each year, perhaps seventeen or so in the early Empire. Other Roman cities with racing facilities held chariot races more or less often, depending on what they could afford. As might be expected, those financed by the emperor and staged in the mighty Circus Maximus were by far the grandest and most prestigious, and they naturally attracted drivers and fans from all over the Mediterranean world.

On a typical day when the Circus Maximus or some other racetrack in the capital featured races, huge crowds jammed the facility. Many no doubt stayed to see all the races, which numbered twenty-four per day by the mid–first century A.D. These spectators were a mix of men, women, freedmen (freed slaves), and slaves, because anyone who could find a place to sit or stand could attend (and admission was free). Because they often watched for many hours at a stretch, spectators often sat on cushions, either carried from home or rented at the circus. Some also periodically snacked on food brought from home or sold by vendors and snack bars located beneath the stands. Besides the spectators of all walks of life and the merchants who catered to them, there were also prostitutes, gamblers, pickpockets, and other such characters

A relief sculpture depicts a series of chariot drivers competing in the Circus Maximus, the Roman Empire's largest and most famous racing facility.

This fanciful depiction of the Roman poet Ovid captures his pleasant manner and urbane charm.

present; the circus was, as Robert Kebric memorably puts it, "literally a meeting place for the Roman world."[73]

Indeed, the following charming passage by the Roman poet Ovid (Publius Ovidius Naso, 43 B.C.–ca. A.D. 17) shows that an exhibition of chariot races was as much a social occasion or a chance to pursue romance as it was a sports spectacle.

> I'm not sitting here because of my enthusiasm for horse races; but I will pray that the chariot driver you favor may win. I came here, in fact, so that I might sit beside you and talk to you. I didn't want the love which you stir in me to be concealed from you. So, you watch the races, and I'll watch you. Let's each watch the things we love most, and let's feast our eyes on them. Oh, how lucky is the chariot driver you favor! Does he have the good fortune to attract your attention? Let me, please, have that good fortune. . . . Why are you edging away from me? It's no use. The seat marker forces us to touch. Yes, the Circus does offer some advantages in its seating rules. Hey, you on the right, whoever you are, be more considerate of the lady! . . . Draw in your legs, if you have any sense of decency, and don't stick your bony knees in her back. Oh dear, your skirt is trailing a bit on the ground. Lift it up, or here, I will do it. . . . Would you like me to stir a light breeze by using my program as a fan? . . . Good, the track is clear and ready for the first big race. . . . I can see the driver you're cheering for. I'm sure he'll win. Even his horses seem to know what you want. Oh no, he's swinging [too] wide around the turning post. What are you doing? The driver in second position is coming up from behind. Pull on the left rein with your strong hand! . . . Oh, we're cheering for an idiot and a coward. . . . The starting gates are open again, the horses break, and the different-colored teams fly onto the track. Now, gallop ahead and take a clear lead! Fulfill my girlfriend's hopes, and my own. (Good! Her wishes have been granted, [while] mine remain to be granted. . . . Ah, she smiled, and promised me something with her sly eyes.)[74]

Factions, Colors, Fans, and Partisans

Ovid's mention of "different-colored teams" is a reference to rival racing organizations, or factions (*factiones*), one of the more important social, as well as economic, aspects of the races. A *factio* was a private stable run by a businessman, a *dominus factionis* (plural, *domini factionum*), who hired out his horses, equipment, and drivers (many of whom were slaves and therefore his property) to the government magistrate who financed and supervised the races. In a way, the *domini factionum* are comparable to modern owners of professional football and other sports teams. They grew rich from collecting not only their rental fees but also the often considerable prize money for winning races. (The owners then paid the drivers, who were viewed essentially as hired hands, much smaller sums for their services.)

Each faction was identified by the color of the tunics its drivers wore. The four traditional colors—the Whites, Reds, Blues, and Greens—were very ancient, dating back perhaps to the days of the kings. There were no factions in that early period. The probable development was: first, the drivers wearing these colors became fan favorites, prompting the perpetuation of loyal fan support for the colors; over time the rivalry between the four colors became fierce; and later, when actual racing organizations emerged in the early first century A.D., each fan following came to identify itself with a faction and vice versa. Some scholars suggest that the first two formal stables were the Reds and Whites, followed by the Blues and Greens.[75] (As time went on, even though there remained four factions, each with its charioteers wearing a distinctive color, the fans tended to divide their allegiance mostly between the two most popular—the Greens and Blues.)

A charioteer stands with one of his horses in this mosaic. Each racing stable (factio) *had several drivers and teams.*

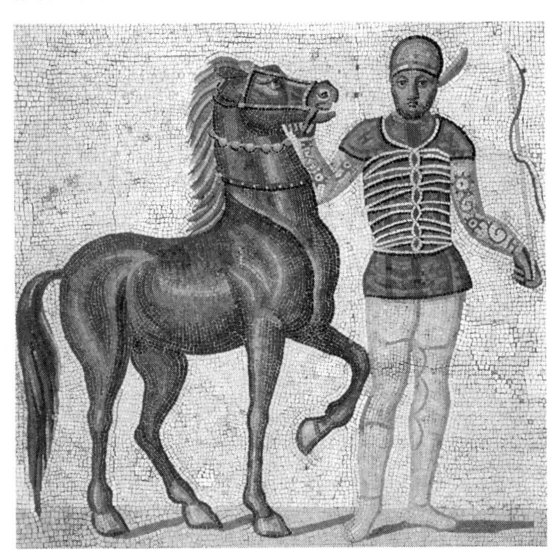

Both the differences and connections between the racing stables and their fans are further complicated by the common misidentification of the term *factiones* with racing partisans. Besides its regular fan following from the general population, each color/faction had a hard-core group of devotees—the partisans. Relatively few in number (perhaps fewer than a thousand for each color in each major city), the partisans formed clubs, sat and loudly cheered together in the circus, likely socialized together, and sometimes received the financial support of wealthy individuals seeking to bolster the images of their favorite colors. But the partisans usually had no formal connections with the stables and owners themselves.

Partisan Allegiance and Violence

Whether given by partisans or ordinary fans, public allegiance for the factions was often intense, and sometimes even fanatical, as it is today among the supporters of national soccer teams at the World Cup competitions. In a letter to a friend, Pliny the Younger, who held himself intellectually above the "childish passions" of the racing scene, commented on such zealous devotion to colors:

> If they [the fans] were attracted by the speed of the horses or the drivers' skill one could account for it, but in fact it is the racing-colors they really support and care about, and if the colors were to be exchanged in mid-course during a race, they would transfer their favor and enthusiasm and rapidly desert the famous drivers and horses whose names they shout as they recognize them from afar. Such is the popularity of a worthless shirt—I don't mean with the crowd, which is worth less than the shirt, but with certain serious individuals. When I think of how this futile, tedious, monotonous business can keep them sitting endlessly in their seats, I take pleasure in the fact that their pleasure is not mine.[76]

Juvenal made the same point more humorously. Here he compares fan reaction to a team's loss to the aftermath of the Battle of Cannae, the worst military defeat Rome ever suffered:

> If I may say so without offense to that countless mob, all Rome is in the Circus today. The roar that assails my eardrums means, I am pretty sure, that the Greens have won—otherwise you'd see such gloomy faces, such sheer astonishment as greeted the Cannae disaster, after our consuls had bitten the dust.[77]

Later, in the sixth century, rivalry between the Blues and Greens became so intense in Constantinople (Rome's eastern capital, which had survived the fall of the western Empire) that their supporters often attacked and even killed one another. According to the Byzantine historian Procopius (ca. A.D. 500–ca. 563):

> At first they were destroying their rival partisans, but as time went on they began to slay also those who had given them no offense at all. . . . And these things took place no longer in darkness or concealment, but at all hours of the day . . . for the wrongdoers had no need to conceal their crimes, for no dread of punishment lay on them.[78]

By 532, sporadic violence between Blues and Greens partisans had escalated so far that it forced the emperor Justinian (reigned 527–565) to arrest several leading partisans. This action touched off a citywide riot that almost destroyed the capital. The magnificent church of St. Sophia, part of the imperial palace, and other buildings were burned as angry crowds rampaged, screaming "*Nika!*" (Victory!), the name by which the rebellion came to be known. Eventually Justinian unleashed his capable general Belisarius, whose troops attacked the rioters, killing some thirty thousand of them.

The Drivers and Their Chariots

Of course, such intense rivalry among the supporters of the various racing colors was matched by that among the charioteers who represented their respective stables on the racetrack itself. Though they had to do the bidding of the stable owners and suffered some of the same social discrimination as gladiators did, they were still avid team players. Chariot racing was extremely dangerous, yet these drivers usually gave it their all, risking their lives to beat their opponents and thereby to heap prestige and money on their home stables (and their owners).

These athletes were also motivated by the chance, however small it may have been, to

The mosaic depicts a four-horse chariot (quadrigarum) *during its victory lap after winning a race. The charioteer waves at his fans, while another man (perhaps the faction owner) proudly carries the victory palm.*

gain both fame and money for themselves. Winning charioteers sometimes became widely popular sports figures, even though most began as slaves. Some became "like movie stars today," Jo-Ann Shelton points out, "recognized as they walked down the streets of Rome and greeted with swoons and squeals of delight."[79] Although the owners received the purses, or prize money, they did pay the drivers. And successful charioteers eventually gained their freedom (if they did start out as slaves) and began receiving larger percentages of the purse. It was not unheard-of, therefore, for popular drivers to become rich men. According to Juvenal, "You'll find that a hundred lawyers scarcely make more than one successful jockey."[80] And Martial asked with a touch of bitterness:

> How long shall I be a caller [i.e., call on his patron and receive pocket money for doing him favors], earning a hundred coppers in a whole day . . . when Scorpus [one of the more celebrated charioteers] in a single hour carries off as winner fifteen heavy bags of gold hot from the mint?[81]

Scorpus, who won more than 2,000 races and died in a track accident at age twenty-six, was only one of several successful charioteers mentioned in ancient writings or inscriptions. The inscription on a monument erected by one of them, Calpurnianus, tells how he won 1,127 victories, including several that paid him 40,000 *sesterces* (about forty times the annual wage of an average Roman soldier) or more. Another popular charioteer, Crescens, began racing at age thirteen and died at age twenty-four, earning over 1.5 million *sesterces* in his short but glorious career. One of the most remarkable records was that of Diocles, who also set up his own monument, recording the following facts for posterity:

> He drove four-horse chariots for 24 years. He had 4,257 starts, with 1,462 first-place finishes, 110 of them in opening races. In single-entry races, he had 1,064 first-place finishes, winning 92 major purses, 32 of them worth 30,000 *sesterces* . . . 28 of them worth 40,000 *sesterces* . . . 29 worth 50,000 *sesterces* . . . and three worth 60,000 *sesterces*. . . . All total, he was in the money 2,900 times. . . . In races for two-horse chariots, he had 3 first-place finishes. . . . In 815 races, he took the lead at the start and held it to the end. In 67 races, he came from behind to win.[82]

According to Diocles' inscription, he won most of his victories on four-horse chariots. Called *quadrigae*, these were the most common type of chariot. He also mentions competing occasionally in two-horse versions (*bigae*). Less frequently seen, although not rare, were races for chariots with three horses (*trigae*), six (*seiuges*), eight (*octoiuges*), and even ten (*decemiuges*). Another race staged only occasionally was the *pedibus ad quadrigam*, in which two men stood in the chariot; when the vehicle crossed the finish line, one of them jumped out and sprinted once around the course to determine the winner of the race.

A typical racing chariot, pictured here, was small, lightweight, and required great skill to drive.

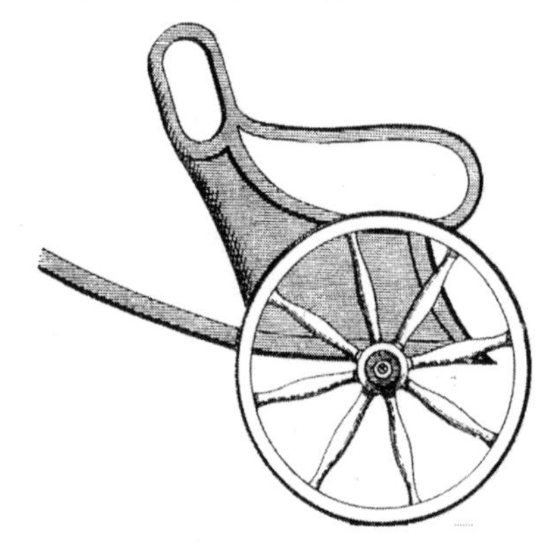

Contests among chariots and teams like these were the main attraction of Roman racing exhibitions. The programs featured no regular horse races—that is, with a jockey riding a horse (as Greek racing did, along with chariot races). The nearest equivalent were the *desultorii*, who probably entertained the circus crowds in the intervals between the chariot races. More of an acrobat than a rider, a *desultor* mounted the backs of two horses that were reined together and performed various tricks, such as handstands or leaps from one horse to the other.

Ruthlessly Vying for the Advantage

An exhibition of chariot racing began with a *pompa*, which in many ways resembled the triumph of a Roman general. Such parades must have varied in size and splendor from city to city and time to time; in Rome, at least, the *pompa* bound for the Circus Maximus started on the sacred Capitoline Hill and wound its way down into and through the Forum before reaching its destination. As Roland Auguet describes it:

> At its head, in a magnificent chariot, came the magistrate who had given the games. . . . He was clothed in a purple toga, wore a tunic embroidered with palms and held . . . the ivory scepter topped by an eagle [symbol of Roman power]; a slave standing behind him held a golden crown over his head. He was surrounded by the gilded youth of Rome, who advanced on horseback, or on foot. . . . Then came the charioteers in their chariots. An incongruous procession of statues, behind

which marched priests and consuls, closed the parade. . . . Tradition had it that . . . when the procession entered the Circus the spectators looked anxiously at the statue of the god who presided over their activities. If, as it passed them [as it was carried in the parade], it made a sign with its head, caused by some movement of its bearers, this would be interpreted as support for their [personal] plans or as promising fulfillment of their desires.[83]

When it was time for the first race to begin, four drivers, each usually (but not necessarily always) representing one of the four traditional colors, underwent a lottery. (Four new drivers held their own lottery prior to the second race, and so forth. Four per race was standard in most circuses. But in a facility the size of the Circus Maximus, there was room for up to twelve contestants per race, in which case each faction might be represented by three drivers, who helped one another during the race to ensure victory for their stable.) The lottery was determined by placing four different-colored balls in an urn and overturning it, allowing the balls to fall randomly into four bowls. Each bowl represented one of four starting positions: the first against the track's central spine (*euripus*), the next two in the middle, and the last on the outside against the stands.

Then the drivers took their positions and a sudden hush fell over the crowded facility. From his box, located just above the starting gates, the games magistrate tossed out a white cloth (*mappa*); as it touched the track, attendants released a cord that held the fronts of the gates in place and the chariots sprang forward, initiating the race. The drivers had to complete seven full laps (about two and a half miles), during which time they desperately and ruthlessly vied for every possible advantage. Each attempted to maneuver into the inside lane, against the *euripus*, since the distance of a lap in this position was somewhat shorter than in the outer lanes. And often the men tried to sabotage one another by breaking rival wheels or axles or by other nefarious means.

The most spectacular result of such on-track warfare was the "shipwreck" (*naufragium*), in which a chariot and its horses crashed, creating a mass of twisted debris and broken bones. On occasion the chariot would crash but the horses would continue on, dragging the driver along the track. To escape from either of these predicaments, the driver drew a dagger at the last moment and tried to cut himself free of the reins, which wound around his waist, binding him to the horses. If he failed to free himself, he usually suffered injury or death.[84]

Consentius: The Inspiration for Judah Ben-Hur

The most detailed and vivid surviving ancient account of a Roman chariot race is that penned by the fifth-century A.D. Roman poet Sidonius Apollinaris. There were four chariots in the race, one of which was driven by his close friend Consentius and another by one of Consentius's stablemates. This excerpt from the exciting narrative begins with the teams huddled expectantly at the starting gates:

> The four team colors are clearly visible: white and blue, green and red. Grooms are holding the heads and the bridles of the horses . . . calming them with soothing pats and reassuring them with words of encouragement. . . . A shrill blast of the trumpet, and the chariots leap out of the gates, onto the track. . . . The wheels fly over the ground, and the air is choked

with the dust stirred up on the track. . . . The drivers urge their horses with whips. Standing in the chariots, they lean far forward so that they can whip even the shoulders of the horses. . . . The chariots fly out of sight [i.e., behind the *euripus*], quickly covering the long open stretch. . . . When they have come around the far turn, both the rival teams have passed Consentius, but his partner is in the lead. The middle teams concentrate now on taking the lead in the inside lane. . . . Consentius, however, redoubles his efforts to hold back his horses and skillfully reserve their energy for the seventh and last lap. The others race full out, urging their horses with whip and voice. . . . And thus they race, the first lap, the second, the third, the fourth. In the fifth lap the leader is no longer able to withstand the pressure of his pursuers. He knows his horses are exhausted, that they can no longer respond to his demand for speed, and he pulls them aside. When the sixth lap had been completed . . . Consentius's opponents thought they had a very safe lead for the seventh and last lap. . . . But suddenly he loosens the reins, plants his feet firmly on the floorboard, leans far over the chariot . . . and makes his fast horses gallop full out. One of the other drivers tries to make a very sharp turn at the far post, feeling Consentius close on his heels, but he is unable to turn his four wildly excited horses, and they plunge out of control. Consentius passes him carefully. The fourth driver is enthralled by the cheers of the spectators and turns his galloping horses too far right toward the stands. Consentius drives straight and fast and passes [him]. . . . The latter pursues Consentius recklessly, hoping to overtake him. He cuts in sharply across the track. His horses lose their balance and fall. Their legs become tangled in the spinning chariot wheels and are snapped and broken. The driver is hurled headlong out of the shattered chariot which then falls on top of him in a heap of twisted wreckage. His broken and bloody body is still [i.e., he is dead]. And now the emperor presents the palm branch of victory to Consentius.[85]

This account undoubtedly provided American diplomat and writer Lew Wallace (1827–1905) with much of his inspiration for the great chariot race he depicted in his famous 1880 novel, *Ben-Hur*. The book was itself the inspiration for two spectacular films (released in 1925 and 1959, respectively). The on-track duel between Consentius and his opponent, the opponent's crash and death, and Consentius's subsequent victory are all closely paralleled in Wallace's version. The hero, Judah Ben-Hur, a Jew who had earlier served as a galley slave, is pursued and harassed along the racecourse by his friend-turned-enemy, the Roman driver Messala. But with less than a lap left in the contest, Messala's chariot capsizes, allowing Ben-Hur to win the palm.

Consentius and his opponents, along with their entire civilization, passed away long ago, of course. Yet in a way, through the on-screen exploits of Wallace's charioteers, they still live on, repeatedly recapturing the thrills and spills of Rome's favorite sport for eager new generations.

The Games in Decline

It is possible that all of the popular Roman games (except for the *naumachiae*, because of their tremendous expense) might have maintained their popularity and continued to be held right up till the last gasps of Roman civilization. However, something momentous occurred in the fourth century that changed the face of the public shows. This was the amazingly swift rise and political (as well as religious) triumph of Christianity. Despite periodic persecutions from the first century on, the faith had persisted and slowly grown in popularity. Then, in the early fourth century, the Christians received two major boosts: the first in 313 when the emperor Constantine (reigned 307–337) issued an edict granting them religious freedom, and the second in 337 when he converted to Christianity on his deathbed. Thereafter, all but one of Rome's emperors were Christians, and an increasing number of Roman pagans (non-Christians) converted.[86]

The Christians viewed the gladiatorial games as both murder and an offense against humanity. And leading Christian spokesmen increasingly came to condemn the *munera*. They often cited Tertullian, who had earlier harshly denounced both the gladiator's art and the arena spectators:

> He who shudders at the body of a man who died by nature's law . . . will, in the amphitheater, gaze down with most tolerant eyes on the bodies of men mangled, torn to pieces, defiled with their own blood; yes, and he who comes to the spectacle to signify his approval of

The Roman emperor Constantine witnesses a glowing cross in the sky on the day before a crucial battle. Interpreting the cross as a Christian emblem, he later supported the Christians.

> murder being punished, will have a reluctant gladiator hounded on with lash and rod to do murder.[87]

In the last half of the fourth century a large proportion of Romans were still pagans, most of whom wanted gladiatorial games to continue. But they eventually had to give in to the increasing political power of the Christians, who had come to control the government. At the urgings of Christian bishops like Ambrose (Ambrosius Aurelius, ca. 340–397), the emperor Theodosius I (reigned 392–395) banned the worship of the old Roman gods in favor of the Christian god. By the end of the fourth century the gladiator schools had been closed; and perhaps about thirty or forty years later, the last actual gladiatorial fights took place in the Colosseum.

Some Games Survive

Despite the demise of gladiatorial contests, other public games survived for a considerable time. The execution of criminals and the *venationes* continued to be held for at least another century. Surviving writings reveal that as late as 523, half a century after the last Roman emperor had been driven from his throne, the Colosseum still drew huge crowds to watch animal hunts and wrestling matches. Rome was still a large and vital city, after all, and much of Italy remained prosperous under the leadership of the humane and capable Theodoric the Ostrogoth, who ruled the shrunken remnants of the western Empire from 493 to 526. Theodoric's Latin secretary, Cassiodorus (ca. 490–ca. 585), praised and sympathized with the still popular animal hunter,

> for his endeavors to please the people, who, after all, are secretly hoping to see him killed. And what a horrible death he dies—denied even the rites of burial, disappearing before he has yet become a corpse into the maw of the hungry animal he has failed to kill![88]

But soon after this period, the city of Rome rapidly declined. Lacking the administration and services the Roman government had provided for so many centuries, it increasingly fell into disrepair and became largely depopulated. There was simply no more government money or administrative apparatus to procure animals and stage spectacles, and huge crowds with the desire and leisure time to attend such games no longer existed in most cities. Indeed, by the end of the sixth century, grass had begun to grow on bleachers of the Colosseum and other amphitheaters, where for so long audiences had loudly cheered and with a turn of their thumbs decreed life or death.

Chariot Racing and Byzantine Court Ceremony

In the wake of the western Empire's disintegration, the Circus Maximus and other Roman racetracks in the west were also abandoned, and they began slowly but steadily to accumulate debris and fade from sight. However, chariot racing survived for several more centuries in the Empire's eastern sector, which became the Greek Byzantine Empire. It was in Constantinople's great racetrack, in 532, that thousands of the rioters in the so-called Nika revolt were slaughtered by Justinian's order.

In fact, well before Justinian's time the government's presentation of chariot races had become a potent tool for the glorification and consolidation of imperial power. By the

The once splendid Colosseum rises behind the ruins of smaller Roman structures. The mighty Roman Empire disintegrated in the fifth and sixth centuries, leaving its amphitheaters and circuses empty and crumbling.

fourth century, says Alan Cameron, the circus (which usually closely adjoined the palace) had evolved into

> a backdrop against which the emperor could act out in due pomp his role as divine ruler, victor in war, and provider of peace, plenty, and games. So effective and popular a part of the emperor's public *persona* had this performance become that a circus was evidently felt to be as indispensable to the [rulers] as a palace.[89]

For this reason, the Byzantine court maintained large-scale chariot races for hundreds of years. Meanwhile, the circus partisans also came to reinforce the imperial image. In the sixth and seventh centuries, groups of Blues and Greens became permanent members of the court and its complex ceremonies (at the same time, apparently, greatly reducing the threat of their rioting). They not only attended the races, where they performed formal cheers and songs for the emperor, but also sang chants for him and his family in the throne room, royal processions, and elsewhere.

The Stuff of Legend

In time, however, Byzantine racing declined, just as the other Roman games had. This was because it finally became much too expensive to stage such large-scale spectacles in a realm that was itself in rapid economic and political decline. The last chariot races took place in the late twelfth century or shortly thereafter. The decline of Byzantine civilization then continued, culminating in the sack of Constantinople by the Ottoman Turks in 1453, an event that eliminated the last surviving remnant of the once mighty Roman Empire. In the centuries that followed, as the old amphitheaters and circuses fell further into decay, the fabulous Roman games became, along with their makers, the stuff of legend.

Notes

Introduction: Rome's Favorite Form of Entertainment

1. Sallust, *The Conspiracy of Catiline*, excerpted in *Sallust: The Jugurthine War/The Conspiracy of Catiline*, trans. S. A. Handford. New York: Penguin Books, 1988, p. 220.
2. Carlin A. Barton, *The Sorrow of the Ancient Romans: The Gladiator and the Monster*. Princeton, NJ: Princeton University Press, 1993, pp. 24–25.
3. For this reason, most such performers were slaves or freedmen (freed slaves), although a few freeborn citizens competed for money, glory, or both. On rare occasions, high-born Romans performed in the theater or arena, but as in the notorious cases of the emperors Nero and Commodus, they were usually harshly criticized or ridiculed (behind their backs, of course).
4. David C. Young, *The Olympic Myth of Greek Amateur Athletics*. Chicago: Ares, 1984, p. 173.
5. Quoted in J. P. V. D. Balsdon, *Life and Leisure in Ancient Rome*. New York: McGraw-Hill, 1969, p. 269.

Chapter 1: How the Public Games Originated and Became Popular

6. Cicero, *Tusculan Disputations* 4.33.70, quoted in H. A. Harris, *Sport in Greece and Rome*. Ithaca, NY: Cornell University Press, 1972, p. 53.
7. Plutarch, *Moral Essays* 274d, quoted in Michael B. Poliakoff, *Combat Sports in the Ancient World*. New Haven, CT: Yale University Press, 1987, p. 103.
8. Tacitus, *The Annals*, published as *The Annals of Ancient Rome*, trans. Michael Grant. New York: Penguin, 1989, pp. 322–23.
9. Juvenal, *Satires*, published as *Juvenal: The Sixteen Satires*, trans. Peter Green. New York: Penguin Books, 1974, p. 207.
10. Quoted in Jo-Ann Shelton, ed., *As the Romans Did: A Sourcebook in Roman Social History*. New York: Oxford University Press, 1988, p. 336.
11. Alan Cameron, *Circus Factions: Blues and Greens at Rome and Byzantium*. London: Clarendon Press, 1976, pp. 173–74.
12. This book deals exclusively with the more physical and violent *ludi*, such as chariot races. For a detailed overview of Roman theatricals, see Don Nardo, *Greek and Roman Theater*. San Diego: Lucent Books, 1995.
13. These were the Ludi Megalenses (April 4–10), Ludi Cereales (April 12–19), Ludi Florales (April 28–May 3), Ludi Apollinares (July 6–13), Ludi Romani (September 5–19), and Ludi Plebeii (November 4–17). It should be noted that these were the ones celebrated in the capital city of Rome. Other Roman cities had similar celebrations with their own local variations and flavors.
14. Shelton, *As the Romans Did*, pp. 332–33.
15. See *Life of Caesar*, in Plutarch, *Fall of the Roman Republic: Six Lives by Plutarch*, trans. Rex Warner. New York: Penguin Books, 1972, p. 248.
16. Suetonius, *Julius Caesar*, in Suetonius, *Lives of the Twelve Caesars*, published

as *The Twelve Caesars*, trans. Robert Graves, rev. Michael Grant. New York: Penguin Books, 1979, p. 17.

17. Prologue to Terence, *The Mother-in-Law*, in *Terence: The Comedies*, trans. Betty Radice. New York: Penguin Books, 1976, pp. 293–94.
18. In place of the traditional plays, producers offered more outwardly colorful, and often more vulgar, stage shows, including short, crude farces designed to elicit quick belly laughs; troupes of jugglers, acrobats, sword swallowers, magicians, mind readers, performing animals, and other carnival-like acts; and pantomimes (*fabula saltica*), stories told in music and dance, which were similar to modern ballets.

Chapter 2: Rome's Monumental Games Facilities

19. Edith Hamilton, *The Roman Way to Western Civilization*. New York: W. W. Norton, 1932, p. 116.
20. Vitruvius, *On Architecture*, trans. Frank Granger. 2 vols. Cambridge, MA: Harvard University Press, 1962, vol. 1, p. 255.
21. Tacitus, *The Annals*, Grant translation, p. 188.
22. Quoted in Shelton, *As the Romans Did*, p. 344.
23. Until the mid–first century A.D., a number of the cities in Italy and Rome's provinces that lacked permanent amphitheaters staged gladiatorial bouts and animal shows not only in impermanent wooden structures, but also in small but permanent stone theaters designed primarily for plays and recitations. Ostia (Rome's port) in Italy, Arles and Orange in Gaul (France), and Timgad and Dougga in North Africa, for instance, all had such theaters. In the first century, full-size amphitheaters like (although somewhat smaller than) the Colosseum began to sprout up throughout the realm, eventually numbering seventy-five or more.
24. See *Nero*, in Suetonius, *The Twelve Caesars*, p. 219.
25. *Nero*, in Suetonius, *The Twelve Caesars*, p. 227.
26. The term derived from the Latin word *colosseus*, meaning "colossal."
27. Statius, *Silvae*, in Statius, *Works*, trans. J. H. Mozley. 2 vols. Cambridge, MA: Harvard University Press, 1961, vol. 1, pp. 65–67.
28. Dio Cassius, *Roman History*, quoted in Chris Scarre, *Chronicle of the Roman Emperors*. London: Thames and Hudson, 1995, p. 73.
29. John H. Humphrey, *Roman Circuses: Arenas for Chariot Racing*. Berkeley and Los Angeles: University of California Press, 1986, p. 5.
30. Historians must rely on paintings and other indirect evidence because no Etruscan sports arena has yet been excavated and studied (mainly because these structures were so impermanent that few traces of them have survived).
31. Livy, *The History of Rome from Its Foundation*, excerpted in *Livy: The Early History of Rome*, trans. Aubrey de Selincourt. New York: Penguin Books, 1960, p. 74.
32. It was not one of the famous "seven wonders" of the ancient world, since that list was established by the Greek poet Antipater of Sidon in the second century B.C., long before the Circus Maximus attained its greatest size and splendor.
33. Robert B. Kebric, *Roman People*. Mountain View, CA: Mayfield, 1997, pp. 259–61.

34. Humphrey, *Roman Circuses*, p. 4.
35. Complicating matters somewhat is that archaeologists are sometimes not sure whether they have found the remains of a circus or a stadium, which was in many ways structurally similar to a circus. Although modern writers sometimes refer to both Roman amphitheaters and circuses as stadiums, as a sort of generic term for sports facilities, technically the stadium was a separate kind of facility in its own right. The chief differences between circuses and stadiums were that stadiums were used for general Greek-style athletic games, including, but not primarily, horse and chariot races; they were considerably smaller, having an arena one *stade* (about 600 feet) in length; and they had no stone barrier (*euripus*) dividing the arena floor into two sections.

Chapter 3: Gladiators: Their Public Image, Lives, and Training

36. Calpurnius Flaccus, *Declamatio*, quoted in Barton, *Sorrow of the Ancient Romans*, p. 12.
37. See, for example, Juvenal's sixth satire (lines 345–56, in Green translation, pp. 139–40), and eighth satire (lines 172–200, pp. 183–84).
38. Juvenal, *Satires*, p. 136.
39. Tacitus, *The Annals*, p. 360.
40. Epigram 5.24, in Martial, *Epigrams*, ed. and trans. D. R. Shackleton Bailey. 3 vols. Cambridge, MA: Harvard University Press, 1993, vol. 1, pp. 377–79.
41. Cicero, *Tusculan Disputations*, quoted in Barton, *Sorrow of the Ancient Romans*, p. 18.
42. Seneca, *On Providence*, quoted in Moses Hadas, trans. and ed., *The Stoic Philosophy of Seneca*. New York: W. W. Norton, 1958, pp. 37–38.
43. Tertullian, *On the Spectacles*, quoted in Barton, *Sorrow of the Ancient Romans*, p. 12.
44. Quoted in Shelton, *As the Romans Did*, p. 345. Though theoretically still free during their tenures as gladiators, such volunteers nevertheless had to endure temporarily both a reduction in status, to that of a slave, and the rigors of what was essentially a convict's life.
45. There was, however, a curious double standard regarding those who kept and trained gladiators. While a *lanista*, who made his sole living at it, was scorned, the reputation of an upper-class Roman who maintained a gladiatorial troupe as only a sideline or subsidiary source of income remained unblemished.
46. For a long time, slaves had no choice but to obey their masters and become gladiators. In the second century, however, the enlightened emperor Hadrian modified the law, requiring a master either to get a slave's consent to become a gladiator or to show proof that the slave had committed a crime serious enough to warrant condemnation to the arena.
47. Roland Auguet, *Cruelty and Civilization: The Roman Games*. London: Routledge, 1994, p. 158.
48. Plutarch, *Life of Crassus*, in Plutarch, *Fall of the Roman Republic*, p. 122.
49. Michael Grant, *Gladiators*. New York: Delacorte Press, 1967, pp. 49–50.

Chapter 4: Gladiators: Their Mortal Combats

50. Quoted in Auguet, *Cruelty and Civilization*, p. 80.
51. Auguet, *Cruelty and Civilization*, p. 44.
52. Auguet, *Cruelty and Civilization*, pp. 56–58.

53. Martial, *Epigrams*, vol. 1, pp. 33–35.
54. Petronius, *The Satyricon*, trans. J. P. Sullivan. New York: Penguin Books, 1977, pp. 59–60.
55. Quoted in Auguet, *Cruelty and Civilization*, p. 53.
56. See *Caligula*, in Suetonius, *The Twelve Caesars*, p. 169.
57. Martial, *Epigrams*, vol. 1, p. 19.
58. Seneca, *Moral Letters*, quoted in Hadas, *Stoic Philosophy of Seneca*, p. 172.
59. Cicero, *Letters to His Friends*, quoted in Shelton, *As the Romans Did*, pp. 246–47.

Chapter 5: Wild Animal Shows and Staged Naval Battles

60. Pliny the Elder, *Natural History*, excerpted in *Pliny the Elder: Natural History: A Selection*, trans. John H. Healy. New York: Penguin Books, 1991, pp. 108–109.
61. Pliny the Elder, *Natural History*, p. 112.
62. Plutarch, *Life of Brutus*, in Plutarch, *Makers of Rome: Nine Lives by Plutarch*, trans. Ian Scott-Kilvert. New York: Penguin Books, 1988, p. 230.
63. Cicero, *Letters to His Friends*, quoted in Shelton, *As the Romans Did*, pp. 347–48.
64. Martial, *Epigrams*, vol. 1, p. 25.
65. Martial, *Epigrams*, vol. 1, p. 27.
66. Martial, *Epigrams*, vol. 1, p. 23.
67. Cicero, *Letters to His Friends*, quoted in Shelton, *As the Romans Did*, p. 347.
68. Pliny the Elder, *Natural History*, pp. 111–12. Pliny's mention of Pompey's suffering the effects of the crowd's curses referred to the fact that a few years later, on landing in Egypt, he was treacherously murdered by the boy-king Ptolemy XIII, Cleopatra's brother (see Don Nardo, *The Collapse of the Roman Republic*. San Diego: Lucent Books, 1998, pp. 38–40). In the same connection, after the pitiless slaughter of the elephants at Pompey's games, a rumor spread far and wide that when the beasts were first captured, they had been promised that once they had entertained the humans they would be allowed to return to their homeland unhurt. Those Romans who accepted this story believed that Pompey betrayed the beasts by slaughtering them and that his own untimely death was a manifestation of the elephants' revenge.
69. Balsdon, *Life and Leisure in Ancient Rome*, pp. 310–11.
70. Martial, *Epigrams*, vol. 1, p. 31.
71. Augustus, *Res gestae*, quoted in Naphtali Lewis and Meyer Reinhold, eds., *Roman Civilization: Sourcebook II: The Empire*. New York: Harper and Row, 1966, p. 16.
72. Tacitus, *The Annals*, p. 277.

Chapter 6: The Circus Charioteers and Their Fans

73. Kebric, *Roman People*, p. 263.
74. Ovid, *Love Affairs*, quoted in Shelton, *As the Romans Did*, pp. 352–54.
75. Domitian established two more colors—the Golds and Purples—in the late first century, but they failed to gain a following and faded from view fairly quickly.
76. Pliny the Younger, *Letters*, excerpted in *The Letters of the Younger Pliny*, trans. Betty Radice. New York: Penguin Books, 1969, p. 236.
77. Juvenal, *Satires*, pp. 233–34. In the Cannae battle, fought in southeastern Italy in 216 B.C., Hannibal, the great Carthaginian general, crushed a Roman army commanded by the consuls Varro and Paullus. More than fifty thousand Romans died.
78. Procopius, *The Secret History*, in Procopius, *Works*, trans. H. B. Dewing. 7 vols.

Cambridge, MA: Harvard University Press, 1961, vol. 6, pp. 77–79, 85.

79. Shelton, *As the Romans Did*, p. 359.
80. Juvenal, *Satires*, p. 167.
81. Martial, *Epigrams*, vol. 2, p. 393.
82. Quoted in Shelton, *As the Romans Did*, p. 356.
83. Auguet, *Cruelty and Civilization*, pp. 126–27.
84. Pliny the Elder mentions the unusual occurrence (at races given by Claudius) of a driver for the Whites being thrown from his chariot near the start of the race. His horses continued on for the whole seven laps and carried the driverless rig across the finish line ahead of the other teams. Pliny does not say whether this was legally allowed to stand as a win for the Whites. See *Natural History*, p. 122.
85. Sidonius Appolinaris, *Poems*, quoted in Shelton, *As the Romans Did*, pp. 351–52.

Epilogue: The Games in Decline

86. Julian, who ruled from 361 to 363, attempted to de-emphasize Christianity in favor of Rome's "pagan" traditions, but he met with opposition and also died young, leaving his successors to reverse his policies and support the Christians.
87. Tertullian, *Apology*, quoted in Peter Quennell, *The Colosseum*. New York: Newsweek Book Division, 1971, p. 75.
88. Quoted in Quennell, *The Colosseum*, p. 82.
89. Cameron, *Circus Factions*, p. 182.

Glossary

aedile: In republican times, a Roman public official who supervised public buildings, markets, and entertainments, including the games.

amphitheater (in Latin, *amphitheatrum*, meaning "double theater"): A wooden or stone structure, usually oval shaped and open at the top, in which the ancient Romans staged public games and shows, especially gladiatorial fights.

andabates: Gladiators who fought while blindfolded by helmets with no eyeholes.

bestiarius (plural, *bestiarii*)**:** "Beast-man"; an arena hunter who may have had a lower status or used a different fighting style than a *venator*.

bigae: Two-horse chariots.

carceres: The starting gates in a Roman circus.

cavea: The seating complex of a Roman theater, amphitheater, or circus.

circus*:* A long wooden or stone structure in which the ancient Romans staged horse and chariot races; the most famous example was the Circus Maximus in Rome.

damnatio ad ludum: "Condemned to the gladiator barracks"; an ancient Roman penalty sometimes inflicted, in lieu of immediate execution, for serious crimes such as arson or treason.

damnatus: Damned, or doomed.

desultorii (singular, *desultor*)**:** Acrobats who performed on the backs of moving horses, probably during the intervals between chariot races in the circus.

dictata: Lessons, rules, or orders.

dignitas: Dignity.

dimachaeri: Gladiators who fought without shields, using two swords, one in each hand.

doctores: "Teachers"; trainers of gladiators and other arena fighters.

domini factionum: Owners of the circus factions.

equites: Gladiators who fought on horseback.

essedarii: Gladiators who fought from moving chariots.

euripus (or *spina*)**:** The long, narrow, highly ornamented barrier running down the middle of a Roman racetrack.

factions (in Latin, *factiones*; singular *factio*)**:** Private stables or racing organizations that supplied drivers, horses, and equipment for the circus games.

feriae: Traditional religious festivals in ancient Rome.

hoplomachus: A kind of gladiator, either the same as or very similar to a Samnite.

importunus: Rude or crude.

infamia: "Bad reputation"; a social stigma shared by Roman actors, gladiators, and other public performers.

lanista: A professional supplier of gladiators.

laquearii: Gladiators whose principal weapon was the lasso.

ludi (singular, *ludus*)**:** Public games and shows in ancient Rome, including *ludi circenses* (chariot races), *ludi magni* (games held to celebrate a military victory), and *ludi scaenici* (theatrical plays); also, schools where arena fighters trained, including *ludi bestiariori* (schools for animal fighters) and *ludi gladiatori* (schools for gladiators).

maeniana (singular, *maenianum*): Separate seating zones in the *cavea* of a Roman amphitheater.

mappa: A napkin or handkerchief; a white one was thrown by the games magistrate to signal the start of a chariot race.

Morituri te salutant!: "Those about to die salute you!"; the phrase recited by gladiators just prior to combat.

munera (singular, *munus*)**:** "Offerings"; public shows involving gladiators.

munerarius (or *editor*) The magistrate, or public official, in charge of the amphitheater shows.

myrmillo (or *murmillo*)**:** "Fishman"; a kind of gladiator, similar to a Samnite but less heavily armored.

naufragium: "Shipwreck"; in a chariot race, a crashed chariot, usually including its team and sometimes its driver.

naumachia (plural, *naumachiae*)**:** A staged sea battle.

noxii ad gladium ludi damnati: "Condemned to be killed by the sword in the games"; a death sentence to be carried out in the arena.

obscaenus: Indecent, filthy, or loathsome.

odium generis humani: "Hatred for the human race"; the attitude the Romans mistakenly attributed to the early Christians.

palus: A six-foot-tall wooden pole used by gladiatorial trainees as a stand-in for an opponent.

panem et circenses: "Bread and circuses"; an informal term for the Roman government policy of distributing free food to the urban masses while heavily subsidizing the public games and shows.

parma: A small round shield used by Thracian warriors and gladiators.

pedibus ad quadrigam: A chariot race in which two men rode in a chariot; near the end of the race, one man dismounted and ran a lap on foot.

perditus: Hopeless, ruined, or lost.

podium: A seating section in a Roman amphitheater, consisting of a flat marble terrace running around the lower portion of the *cavea*, reserved for royalty or high-ranking officials.

pompa: The parade like ceremony that opened gladiatorial fights, chariots races, and other spectacles.

primus palus: The most skilled and feared group of gladiators in a barracks; the *secundus palus* was the second best, and so on.

probatio armorum: The inspection of gladiators' weapons just prior to combat.

pulvinar: "Royal box"; in an amphitheater, the seating section reserved for the emperor and his family.

quadrigae: Four-horse chariots.

retiarius (plural, *retiarii*)**:** "Net-wielder"; a kind of gladiator who wore no armor and carried a net and a long trident.

sagittarii: Arena fighters who used bows and arrows to slaughter animals.

Samnite: A member of a fierce central Italian hill tribe conquered by the Romans during the early Republic, or a kind of gladiator attired as a Samnite warrior—heavily armored and carrying a sword and heavy shield.

scutum: The rectangular shield carried by Roman soldiers and also by certain gladiators, including the *myrmillo* and Samnite.

secutor: A kind of gladiator, either the same as or very similar to a Samnite.

sica: A curved short sword wielded by Thracian warriors and gladiators.

sine missione: "To the death"; a kind of gladiatorial combat in which the combatants had to continue fighting until one was killed.

stans missus: Condition of a gladiator who attained a draw.

taurarii: Arena fighters who specialized in fighting and killing bulls.

Thracians (in Latin, *Thraces*)**:** Natives of the northern Greek region of Thrace, or gladiators attired as Thracian warriors—lightly armored and carrying a curved sword and small round shield.

unctores: Masseurs.

velarium: A huge awning spread across the open space at the top of a Roman theater or amphitheater to shield the spectators from the sun.

venationes (singular, *venatio*)**:** "Hunts"; various kinds of animal shows.

venator (plural, *venatores*): "Hunter"; an arena performer who fought and killed animals.

verabulum: A hunting spear.

vivarium: A game preserve, or a holding area for animals.

For Further Reading

Editor's Note: The following clearly written introductory books provide much useful background information about Roman history, society, culture, games, and spectacles.

Ian Andrews, *Pompeii*. Cambridge, England: Cambridge University Press, 1978.

Isaac Asimov, *The Roman Empire*. Boston: Houghton Mifflin, 1967.

Lionel Casson, *Daily Life in Ancient Rome*. New York: American Heritage, 1975.

Anthony Marks and Graham Tingay, *The Romans*. London: Usborne, 1990.

Susan McKeever, *Ancient Rome*. London: Dorling Kindersley, 1995.

Don Nardo, *The Roman Empire*. San Diego: Lucent Books, 1994.

———, *Greek and Roman Theater*. San Diego: Lucent Books, 1995.

———, *The Age of Augustus*. San Diego: Lucent Books, 1996.

———, *The Collapse of the Roman Republic*. San Diego: Lucent Books, 1998.

———, *The Roman Colosseum*. San Diego: Lucent Books, 1998.

———, *Life of a Roman Slave*. San Diego: Lucent Books, 1999.

Pompeii: The Vanished City. Alexandria, VA: Time-Life Books, 1992.

Judith Simpson, *Ancient Rome*. New York: Time-Life Books, 1997.

Works Consulted

Ancient Sources in Translation

Moses Hadas, trans. and ed., *The Stoic Philosophy of Seneca*. New York: W. W. Norton, 1958.

Juvenal, *Satires*, published as *Juvenal: The Sixteen Satires*. Trans. Peter Green. New York: Penguin Books, 1974.

Naphtali Lewis and Meyer Reinhold, eds., *Roman Civilization: Sourcebook II: The Empire*. New York: Harper and Row, 1966. Contains several English translations of original documents relating to Roman entertainments.

Livy, *The History of Rome from Its Foundation*, excerpted in *Livy: The Early History of Rome*. Trans. Aubrey de Selincourt. New York: Penguin Books, 1960.

———, *Livy: Rome and the Mediterranean*. Trans. Henry Bettenson. New York: Penguin Books, 1976.

Martial, *Epigrams*. Ed. and trans. D. R. Shackleton Bailey. 3 vols. Cambridge, MA: Harvard University Press, 1993.

Petronius, *The Satyricon*. Trans. J. P. Sullivan. New York: Penguin Books, 1977.

Pliny the Elder, *Natural History*, excerpted in *Pliny the Elder: Natural History: A Selection*. Trans. John H. Healy. New York: Penguin Books, 1991.

Pliny the Younger, *Letters*, excerpted in *The Letters of the Younger Pliny*. Trans. Betty Radice. New York: Penguin Books, 1969.

Plutarch, *Parallel Lives*, excerpted in *Fall of the Roman Republic: Six Lives by Plutarch*. Trans. Rex Warner. New York: Penguin Books, 1972. Contains the lives of Marius, Sulla, Crassus, and Pompey.

———, Caesar, and Cicero; also excerpted in *Makers of Rome: Nine Lives by Plutarch*. Trans. Ian Scott-Kilvert. New York: Penguin Books, 1988. Contains the lives of Coriolanus, Fabius Maximus, Marcellus, Cato the Elder, Tiberius Gracchus, Gaius Gracchus, Sertorius, Brutus, and Mark Antony.

Procopius, *Works*. Trans. H. B. Dewing. 7 vols. Cambridge, MA: Harvard University Press, 1961.

Sallust, *The Conspiracy of Catiline*, excerpted in Sallust: *The Jugurthine War/The Conspiracy of Catiline*. Trans. S. A. Handford. New York: Penguin Books, 1988.

Jo-Ann Shelton, ed., *As The Romans Did: A Sourcebook in Roman Social History*. New York: Oxford University Press, 1988. Contains English translations of numerous ancient documents pertaining to Roman leisure activities, including the games and spectacles.

Statius, *Works*. Trans. J. H. Mozley. 2 vols. Cambridge, MA: Harvard University Press, 1961.

Suetonius, *Lives of the Twelve Caesars*, published as *The Twelve Caesars*. Trans. Robert Graves, rev. Michael Grant. New York: Penguin Books, 1979.

Tacitus, *The Annals*, published as *The Annals of Ancient Rome*. Trans. Michael Grant. New York: Penguin Books, 1989.

Terence, complete surviving works in *Terence: The Comedies*. Trans. Betty Radice. New York: Penguin Books, 1976.

Vitruvius, *On Architecture*. Trans. Frank Granger. 2 vols. Cambridge, MA: Harvard University Press, 1962.

Major Modern Sources

Roland Auguet, *Cruelty and Civilization: The Roman Games*. London: Routledge, 1994. A commendable overview of Roman games, including gladiatorial combats, *naumachiae* (staged sea battles), wild beast hunts, chariot races, circus factions, and the layout of circuses and amphitheaters.

J. P. V. D. Balsdon, *Life and Leisure in Ancient Rome*. New York: McGraw-Hill, 1969. This huge, detailed, and masterful volume by a highly respected historian is one of the best general studies of Roman life, customs, and traditions. In addition to sections on exercise, festivals, arena games, wild animal shows, chariot races, and Greek sports (as practiced by the Romans), it contains fulsome discussions of Roman theater, mimes and pantomimes, children's games, family life, schooling, slavery, dining habits, public baths, and more.

Alan Cameron, *Circus Factions: Blues and Greens at Rome and Byzantium*. London: Clarendon Press, 1976. This definitive modern work on Roman racing organizations lays to rest numerous previous mistaken assumptions and conclusions about this fascinating sidelight of the Roman games. Will appeal mainly to scholars.

Michael Grant, *Gladiators*. New York: Delacorte Press, 1967. Although much information about Roman gladiatorial combats can be found in other books, notably those by Auguet, Balsdon, Barton, Carcopino, and Quennell (all cited in this bibliography), as well as various articles in classical journals, this book by Grant, one of the most prolific of modern classical historians, is the most comprehensive and readable general study of the subject.

John H. Humphrey, *Roman Circuses: Arenas for Chariot Racing*. Berkeley and Los Angeles: University of California Press, 1986. This large, scholarly volume, the most comprehensive available study of the construction and use of Roman racing facilities, will appeal mainly to specialists in Roman history and culture.

Vera Olivova, *Sport and Games in the Ancient World*. New York: St. Martin's Press, 1984. This large, well-written volume begins with useful overviews of how experts think that sport originally evolved and of early athletic practices in the Near East and Egypt. The author then examines Greek sports, beginning with the Bronze Age and Homeric depictions, and concludes with Etruscan games and Roman festivals and games.

Michael B. Poliakoff, *Combat Sports in the Ancient World*. New Haven, CT: Yale University Press, 1987. Detailed, well written, and well documented, this is the definitive recent study of ancient wrestling, boxing, pancratium, and other combat sports.

Additional Modern Sources

Jean-Pierre Adam, *Roman Building: Materials and Techniques*. Trans. Anthony Mathews. Bloomington: Indiana University Press, 1994.

Lesley Adkins and Roy A. Adkins, *Handbook to Life in Ancient Rome*. New York: Facts On File, 1994.

Carlin A. Barton, *The Sorrow of the Ancient Romans: The Gladiator and the Monster*. Princeton, NJ: Princeton University Press, 1993.

J. B. Bury, *History of the Later Roman*

Empire. 2 vols. 1923. Reprint, New York: Dover, 1958.

L. Sprague de Camp, *The Ancient Engineers*. New York: Ballantine Books, 1963.

Jerome Carcopino, *Daily Life in Ancient Rome: The People and the City at the Height of the Empire.* New Haven, CT: Yale University Press, 1940. Rev. ed., 1992.

Tim Cornell and John Matthews, *Atlas of the Roman World*. New York: Facts On File, 1982.

F. R. Cowell, *Life in Ancient Rome*. New York: G. P. Putnam's Sons, 1961.

Leonardo B. Dal Maso, *Rome of the Caesars*. Trans. Michael Hollingworth. Rome: Bonechi-Edizioni, n.d.

Michael Grant, *The World of Rome.* New York: New American Library, 1960.

L. A. Hamey and J. A. Hamey, *The Roman Engineers*. Cambridge, England: Cambridge University Press, 1981.

Edith Hamilton, *The Roman Way to Western Civilization*. New York: W. W. Norton, 1932.

H. A. Harris, *Sport in Greece and Rome*. Ithaca, NY: Cornell, University Press, 1972.

Harold Johnston, *The Private Life of the Romans*. New York: Cooper Square, 1973.

Robert B. Kebric, *Roman People*. Mountain View, CA: Mayfield, 1997.

Senatore R. Lanciani, *Ancient and Modern Rome*. New York: Cooper Square, 1963.

William L. MacDonald, *The Architecture of the Roman Empire*. New Haven, CT: Yale University Press, 1982.

Claude Moatti, *In Search of Ancient Rome*. New York: Harry N. Abrams, 1993.

Peter Quennell, *The Colosseum*. New York: Newsweek Book Division, 1971.

Chris Scarre, *Chronicle of the Roman Emperors*. London: Thomas and Hudson, 1995.

Jon Solomon, *The Ancient World in the Cinema*. New York: A.S. Barnes, 1978.

J. B. Ward-Perkins, *Roman Imperial Architecture*. New York: Penguin Books, 1981.

L. P. Wilkinson, *The Roman Experience*. Lanham, MD: University Press of America, 1974.

David C. Young, *The Olympic Myth of Greek Amateur Athletics*. Chicago: Ares, 1984.

Index

Picture Credits

Cover Photo: AKG, London
Archive Photos, 41, 50, 64, 74, 77
Archive Photos/American Stock, 64
©British Museum, 20
Corbis/Archivo Iconografico, S.A., 40, 51, 73
Corbis/Araldo de Luca, 71
Corbis/Bettman, 54 (bottom)
Corbis/© Werner Forman, 30
Corbis/Diego Lezama Orezzoli, 19
Corbis/Gianni Dagli Orti, 10
Corbis/Roger Wood, 48
Dover Publications, 9, 14, 32 (top), 35
Hollingworth Illustrations, 32 (bottom)
©Erich Lessing/Art Resource, 61
Library of Congress, 12, 15, 22, 24, 26, 27, 29, 31, 34, 52, 62, 79
North Wind Picture Archives, 8, 9, 12, 16, 17, 28, 39, 42, 43, 49, 54 (top), 59, 60, 63, 67, 70
Scala/Art Resource, 69

About the Author

Don Nardo has published many volumes about ancient Roman history and culture, including *The Decline and Fall of the Roman Empire, The Punic Wars, The Age of Augustus, Rulers of Ancient Rome, Life of a Roman Slave*, and biographies of Julius Caesar and Cleopatra. Nardo also writes screenplays and teleplays and composes music. He lives in Massachusetts with his wife, Christine, and dog, Bud.